Sink
or Swim

SURVIVING THE ODDS BY DESIGN

LEONA J. HOWARD

ISBN 978-1-64468-563-1 (Paperback)
ISBN 978-1-64468-564-8 (Digital)

Covenant Books, Inc.
11661 Hwy 707
Murrells Inlet, SC 29576
www.covenantbooks.com

Contents

Acknowledgments

To my husband, Dave, for his love, support, caregiving, and unending dedication to me.

To my sister, Sandy, for her love and support in my healing journey.

To my extended family, especially Evelyn, Richard (and Joanie), and Rick Jr. and Carol for their prayers and for keeping in close touch with me. Your offers of assistance did not go unnoticed.

To cousins, Linda, Karen, Janet, and Marcia. You stayed on this roller-coaster ride with me and supported me.

To my dear friend Sandy for tirelessly visiting me at the hospital and assisting me with my personal hygiene.

To my dear friend Melanie for your prayers, concerns, and commitment to traveling this journey with me and making sure I had transportation to chemo.

To my dear friends Mary and Sue for your prayers and phone calls in spite of the fact you had your own journeys to deal with.

To my friends at Grand Haven for their prayers, cards, and kindnesses.

To the management and members at Orland Park Health & Fitness and at Tinley Fitness. You were all so supportive and kind.

To the members of my Parkinson's class who provided so much inspiration to me.

To all those not named individually. You know who you are.

And last, but not least, to my medical team to whom I owe my life.

A big thank you. I am truly blessed!

Who I Am

Have you ever gone to bed excited about an upcoming event or party and find that when you wake in the morning, you dreamt about the fun things that happened at that event or party? Or maybe you just experienced a terrible day, went to sleep angry, and then woke up from a nightmare that involved an incident from that previous day. But it had a very different spin from what reality was. Our lives are like our dreams. We never know what we will dream about just as we never know what life has in store for us. And no matter how hard we try to control our lives, nothing is at it seems just like in our dreams. This is so true of my story.

It is hard to believe that in a matter of twenty-seven months, I have endured three primary cancers, one Whipple surgery with complications, chemotherapy, radiation, all the while continuing in my role as a caregiver and dealing with deep spiritual unrest. These twenty-seven months have felt like an eternity. So, when a friend suggested I write my story, I really didn't know where to begin. I realized that in order for you to understand my journey and, in some small way, relate it to your journey, you would need to understand who I am. I am not offering medical advice or asking you to substitute what I say for that of your medical professionals. As a lay person with no medical experience, I had to rely on the information provided me by my medical team and the Internet. My goal was to better understand all that was being thrown at me. My hope is that in some small way, this will serve as one of many tools in your health journey toolbox so that you can advocate for yourself.

As a youngster, I became very independent at an early age. I think I always knew that I needed to be self-sufficient. We were not rich, and my parents worked hard. I attended Catholic grammar and high schools, and so religion was a very important part of my upbringing. My parents were my example and inspiration. In my senior year of high school, my parents were unable to pay my tuition. So I worked part-time and did what I had to do to complete high school successfully. I was driven and goal-oriented.

We all look for that chapter in our life where responsibilities decrease, disposable income increases, our life becomes our own. Or at least I thought. So let me take you back a bit before my journey began because how I approached my life and the expectations would ultimately play a very important role in how I navigated my journey.

Throughout my life, I enjoyed good health, except for the occasional cold or flu. I was truly blessed. My father lived to one month shy of his ninety-third birthday. My mother was eighty-six when she passed. They lived in their own home until the end and never lost their ability to think or remain mobile. It certainly appeared longevity was in the cards for me, which was all the more reason I wanted to stay active and fit. In the last couple of years of their lives, I stepped in to oversee their medical care. I'm sure there were several medical professionals who were not happy with me during that time, but I needed to make sure they received the care they were entitled to. I would later learn that by being their advocate, I was preparing to be an advocate for myself. At that time though, I merely thought of myself as a good daughter.

In October 1972, I turned nineteen years old. One month later, my husband and I married. Throughout our marriage, we worked hard. Many years, both my husband and I worked long hours and even two jobs. We were focused and never gave up on our goals and dreams of enjoying life in our golden years. It was not easy by any means, but the focus and drive would serve us well later in so many aspects of our lives. We were owing to no one, and everything we had, we worked hard for.

Like many people, by age fifty, I already had my sights set on retirement. I always knew that I wanted to be in the fitness industry when I retired. But I also knew that there were hobbies I wanted to enjoy when my time belonged to me. At age fifty-two, I became a certified scuba diver. At that time, scuba diving was the force behind my ability to quit smoking. And I was an avid smoker for forty years. At age fifty-six, I found my niche in life. I obtained both an aqua aerobics instructor certification followed by a personal trainer certification. My goal was to work with the senior population because I was entering that era of my life. I began teaching classes and training clients part-time in preparation for my retirement. It is such a rewarding feeling to see my hopes and dreams coming to fruition. Everything fell into place as I was certain it would. And I found that I loved working with the senior population.

My husband had retired a little early, and I was jealous. At almost sixty years of age, I decided to take that leap and retire early. There was a penalty for doing so; however, we were both comfortable with the change in income. Besides, I had already established myself locally in the health fitness industry. My new venture not only kept me active but fit as well. What more could I have wanted? I was retired, working part-time in a field I absolutely enjoyed and was passionate about, and scuba diving to my heart's content. I was living the dream!

My sister, who is eleven years older than I, was born with cretinism. As I understood it, an iodine deficiency hindered the development of her brain, and so she was classified as learning disabled. Since I was the only sibling and eleven years younger, my parents always assumed that I would be her caregiver when they passed. Who else was there? It was doubly difficult because my sister wasn't severely learning disabled, yet she did not have the skillset to live on her own; she had no coping skills nor was she able to obtain gainful employment during her lifetime.

Mom passed first on Christmas Day 2008, and fourteen months later, my dad followed. My sister was sixty-seven years old at that time, and the only home she knew was with my parents. So Sandy came to live with my husband and me in a home that was relatively small, with many stairs, and two large dogs soon to be three. I did the best I could to make sure she had her own space; although, it was small. There is no manual titled "101: How to Be a Caregiver" that you can have in your book collection to guide you. Disabilities are unique to each person as are their needs. My mother never sat down with me to share much about my sister's condition. And I never asked. The only comment she ever made was that my sister was easy to please and didn't have big wants or desires. She was simple as were her needs. I accepted that. I was about to learn that there are many prongs to caregiving, and it was not as simple as I thought. A caregiver must provide more than shelter and food. Having married at nineteen years of age and gone from home at such a young age, I realized that I had very little understanding about my sister's disabilities or the meaning of caregiving. Catastrophic illnesses, caregiving, and end-of-life planning were not even distant thoughts when I was young and building my life with my husband.

All the goals I set in my life, be them big or small, I met. Many people believe you make your own luck, and there is some truth to that, with the exception of a few things that only God has a hand in. My life was certain. Everything had a way of coming together. There is a lesson to be learned, and Pema Chodron, an American Tibetan Buddhist nun, said it best: "If you are invested in security and certainty, you are on the wrong planet." Unfortunately, this is a lesson that took me two-thirds of a lifetime to learn. But that's not necessarily a bad thing since we cannot live our lives planning our deaths.

And so, with all the pieces in place, my journey begins.

The Beginning

I'm sure we can all remember our senior year in high school. We could not wait for the year to end—no more running to school every day, sitting in classes hour after hour, having to do homework. It was all so boring. I wanted to spread my wings and start living my life. After my graduation ceremony, we all shared hugs and then went on our way, all beginning our own personal journeys unique to each of us. No two goals were alike.

Each person's journey begins differently no matter what type of cancer or catastrophic illness you may develop. There are certain steps you can take, which are common in the management of your health care journey that will help to keep your head above water. Keeping a journal of medical events that occur in your life will provide you with the information you need to take the steps to advocate for yourself. Knowledge is power, and it is only when you have that knowledge can you assess your body language, recognize and research the signs and symptoms, ask the appropriate questions, partake in deciding your treatment options, and select a medical team that you are confident in. Most important, never lose your faith in God. That is standard operating care no matter what catastrophic illness should befall you.

From mid-2012 to October 2016, I had suffered bouts of extreme middle back pain and stomach pain. Initially, I explained it to myself as being a bad case of indigestion. But as time went on and the occurrences became more frequent, I knew it was something more serious. In fact, in August 2016, the painful bouts escalated, and I began to vomit liver bile. I would get sick early in the morning, vomit, the pain would pass, and I would be on my way to teach aqua aerobics classes. There was no doubt that I needed to seek medical attention. I had a routine blood test scheduled for mid-December 2016 and felt that it would be more convenient for my schedule to wait until then as I was sure something would show up in the blood test results. Again, it would all work out.

I began educating myself by searching the Internet based on my symptoms. As a personal trainer, I already had an inkling that my gallbladder could be the culprit. I was very concerned when these incidents occurred but immediately pushed it aside when the attacks passed. I also learned that I could keep up my personal training and group fitness schedule by eating large amounts of candy. The sugar fix gave me the carbohydrates I needed to sustain my activity level and support my energy level. The lack of healthy food did cause me to slowly lose weight, and people began to notice. I would merely respond that it was due to my more active teaching schedule since retiring.

Friday, October 28, 2016, was an interesting day. We were having new windows installed in our home. My husband stayed with the workers while I met one of my clients for breakfast. I started to have one of my usual attacks in the middle of breakfast. I asked for a "doggy bag" so that I could take the rest of my breakfast home. My client never suspected anything because I was known for eating healthy portions. We paid our bill, and I drove my client home. The only problem was that I was forty minutes from home, and the drive may well have been forty hours. I don't know how I ever made that drive given the amount of pain I was experiencing. Every stop-and-go light was agony. But I did make it home.

The workers were moving along slowly, and my sister really didn't notice anything unusual. As in the past, I believed that if I waited long enough, the pain would all disappear. All I said to my husband was that I felt a little ill. About an hour later, the pain in my back and upper abdomen was escalating. I phoned my doctor's office and asked to speak with a nurse. She asked me several questions, and I explained in great detail what I was feeling. She pleaded with me to get to the emergency room of the nearest hospital as quickly as possible and to please not drive myself.

My husband couldn't drive me because we had no windows in my house, and my sister did not have the authority to act or make decisions on our behalf. My ego came into play, and I was not going to call an ambulance. What was I thinking? So contrary to the nurse's advice, I chose to drive myself. The ride to the emergency room felt so much longer than the fifteen minutes it took. I checked in and was immediately seen by a physician. My blood pressure was extremely high, registering at 174/90. It was definitely pain-induced high blood pressure. I have never been fond of pain medication, but after two and a half hours, I did succumb and received a shot of morphine. My blood pressure returned to 133/60. After several tests and a CT scan, it was determined that I had gallstones and hypokalemia, which is a very low level of potassium in my blood serum. Potassium is a mineral that helps muscles move, provides nutrients that cells need, and assists the nerves so that they can send proper signals. It is especially important for the cells in your heart.

The emergency room physician was wonderful. He explained that my lipase was at 3,398 U/L (units per liter of blood), which is alarmingly high. As I understood it, lipase is a pancreatic enzyme that aids in the digestion of fats. Normal levels are around 20 to 70 U/L. The high level and type of pain was an indication that I had pancreatitis due to the gallstones. Pancreatitis should be taken very seriously as if left untreated can be fatal. Food and liquids were withheld from me. By doing so, the hospital was able get my lipase and amylase, another digestive enzyme, somewhat lower. With nothing to digest, my pancreas did not have to work. My lipase and amylase levels fell to 681 U/L and 617 U/L, respectively. (For informational purposes, normal amylase levels are 25 to 125 U/L.)

Let me take a moment to address personal health insurance and life insurance coverages. We are enjoying longer lives because of the advancements in the medical field. With longevity now being enjoyed by many individuals, the risk for catastrophic illness increases substantially. Unfortunately, we are still in the infant stages of treating the illnesses related to senior years, such as cancer, Parkinson's, multiple sclerosis, etc. I would recommend that everyone review the specifics of their health insurance plans and look at the available benefits as they relate to your treatment if you were to contract a debilitating disease. Do you have to stay within an insurance network? Are you happy with the medical professionals available within that network? Do you have faith in the hospitals that fall within your network? If you feel that you might need to reach out to a medical professional outside of the network of your insurance, what steps do you need to take with your insurance provider to obtain approval to do so as you do not want to negate your coverage? What is your financial responsibility if you need medical treatment outside of your network? Have you made alternate arrangements for those who rely on you for continuing care—that is, children, siblings, aged parents? As for life insurance, you must remember that you can be denied coverage because of preexisting conditions. So if you fail to have appropriate coverage prior to becoming ill, you will not be able to get it later. Unfortunately, we all suffer from arrogance when we are healthy and life is flowing smoothly. Life is not constant, and things can change in an instant. Knowing and understanding your benefits will reduce the stress, which is primary to healing. Having a plan in place for those who rely on you will also reduce your stress.

Because of my insurance, the hospital was considered out-of-network, but they were allowed to keep me under observation and stabilize me until a room opened up at a hospital that was in-network. So twenty-four hours later and after having been stabilized, my insurance company hired a private ambulance service to transport me to an approved hospital. This is not an unusual occurrence, especially if your insurance is an HMO, which mine was. The upside of this transfer was that the medical team that stabilized me had privileges at the approved hospital that I was transferred to, so I did not lose the continuity of care, which would have been a concern to me.

On Monday, October 31, 2016, the doctor performed an endoscopic retrograde cholangiopancreatography procedure (ERCP). This is a very invasive procedure and is used to determine and treat certain problems of the biliary or pancreatic duct systems. Tissue samples can also be obtained during this procedure for biopsy. The ERCP confirmed the initial findings, and my gallbladder was removed the following day, November 1, 2017. Because of how sick I was, my recovery from surgery was difficult. Issues addressed early make such a big difference in your recovery. Your body is so much weaker when you wait and let the illness progress. The hospital also gave me a unit of magnesium and potassium because my levels were too low. The surgeon came to see me after surgery to check on me. He commented that the opening in my bile duct was extremely small and narrow. I questioned him, but he did not see any cause for concern. I do regret not pursuing this further. This is truly a sign of how important self-advocacy is in managing your own health care, which I would discover later.

My total hospital stay between both facilities was seven days. My pancreatic enzyme levels continued to decrease, so I was released. Approximately one week later, I received a call from the surgeon's office advising me that my tissue samples taken from the gallbladder came back negative for cancer. Recovery was estimated to be six weeks although I really progressed quickly. As usual, everything came together with certainty in my healing process. About three months after surgery, my body had returned to normal, and things were looking up. I hadn't felt that great in a long time. It really put everything in perspective. Back to normalcy, or so I thought.

3

The Road to Perdition

As I noted at the beginning of chapter 2, each person's journey begins differently, and symptoms can change in the blink of an eye. Expect nothing, take it a day at a time, and pay attention to what your body is telling you. The body is an extraordinary vessel that is happy when everything works in sync. When a system is failing, your body will let you know, but you have to be able to recognize those signs and distinguish them from your everyday aches and pains and usual discomforts. You have to recognize not only the internal signs but the external ones as well. Here is how my body notified me that things were amiss.

In March 2017, my scalp became itchy. I took notice of it, but with winter coming to an end in the Midwest, dry skin and scalp are not uncommon. This went on for several weeks. By the end of April 2017, every part of my body itched. There were no bumps, hives, or redness. It was so severe that I scratched my skin until it bled, and I was unable to sleep because of the itchiness. I also noticed that my urine became a very dark color, and my stool was soft and gray in color. I phoned the doctor and met with her on May 1. She found it quite unusual that my skin had no rashes or redness, but my home has a large yard, and there is a great deal of wild growth. From a practical point of view, we agreed that I may have gotten into some type of vegetation while walking my dogs, so the initial approach was to treat this as though it were an allergic reaction. I don't have allergies, but our bodies do change as we age. Steroids are the general treatment. I never brought to her attention the change in the color of my urine and stool.

I received a prescription for a one-week dose of steroids, and I took it as prescribed. To my disappointment, nothing improved. My symptoms, in fact, had worsened. Prior to calling my doctor, I did some research on the Internet because thyroid disease does run in my family, and I wanted to see if this could be a possibility. A change in stool consistency and frequency can occur in hyperthyroidism, as well as lumps forming on the thyroid. I did recall that some time prior to the gallbladder removal, I had to have a CT scan and was told I had a nodule on my thyroid. I learned that most people over sixty years of age develop nodules on their thyroid that are harmless. I called the doctor to let her know the steroid did not correct the problem, and I questioned her about thyroid disease. The next step was a blood test that would look at that possibility as well as provide an up-to-date blood panel. On May 9, 2017, I had my blood drawn. Two days later, the doctor phoned me at home and shared that there was no thyroid disease. That was the good news. The bad news was that my lipase levels and liver enzymes were once again elevated. However, since I no longer had a gallbladder, we had to look elsewhere. Now I was extremely worried. I knew in my heart that this was not going to go well.

I obtained a copy of my blood test and went through it. Blood test results will show your level of each enzyme, nutrient, etc., and to the right of that reading, it shows the acceptable normal range. I reviewed the results and highlighted the elevated panels. In an attempt to understand the results, I researched the Internet for explanations. The short, simple version was that my liver was not functioning well. The liver is responsible for many things, one of which is removing acid from the body. When the liver failed to complete this task, the acid tried to exit my body through the biggest organ—my skin. Hence, the severe itching.

In discussing the results with my primary care physician, she advised that it would be necessary to consult with a gastrointestinal specialist who would most likely perform another endoscopic retrograde cholangiopancreatography procedure. As you recall from the previous chapter, this is an endoscopic ultrasound that allows the doctor to obtain tissue samples for testing, as well take a very close look at your digestive system.

I was anxious to get this process moving as we had scuba diving vacation plans already in place for late July. The first step would be a consultation. In order to expedite the appointment process, Dr. Lisa contacted the specialist, and I met with his physician assistant on May 9, 2017. During our meeting, it was explained that the ERCP would be performed in order to determine why my pancreatic levels were elevated and, hopefully, identify the cause. There was a suspicion that the problem would be primary sclerosing cholangitis, which is a disease of the bile ducts that carry digestive liver bile to the small intestine. Several symptoms I had been experiencing could be related to this condition. It is caused by an inflammation of the bile duct system, and the general treatment could be the placement of stents in both the pancreatic and common bile ducts. Most stents that are used initially are geared for short-term placement, with removal in two to three months. There are stents that are made of a material for longer term placement if needed. Some individuals have this procedure done, and the condition is corrected. I was told that others can go a few years having this procedure repeated several times before they see any positive results. My first procedure was scheduled for June 1, 2017.

June 1, 2017: The ERCP was performed. My common bile duct was dilated to 15 mm. The normal size would be approximately 4.1 mm. The pancreatic duct was dilated from 4.5 to 5 mm. The normal size would be 1 to 3.5 mm. The ampulla, which is where the pancreatic and bile ducts connect to the small intestine (also known as ampulla of Vater), was large and nodular. My bile duct was swept to clean debris that was found. The recommendation was to obtain my records from the hospital where I had my gallbladder removed, review those records, and perform another ERCP to do an in-depth evaluation of the bile duct system as well as obtain tissue samples for testing. The date for this second procedure was June 12, 2017.

What's important to note is that I was prescribed a pain medication in the event I experienced any discomfort between the scheduled procedures.

June 12, 2017: During this, my second ERCP, another balloon sweep was performed to again clean the debris in the bile ducts. Tissue samples were taken, and the stents were replaced in both the pancreatic and common bile ducts. The doctor's notes indicated that the next procedure would be dependent upon the tissue sample test results. If no cancer was detected, then my next ERCP would be to remove the stents, and hopefully, all blockage would be cleared, and my digestive system would be back in good working order. If the samples tested positive for cancer, then further discussions would be had as to the course of treatment.

June 14, 2017: The pathology report was issued, and the findings were that the tissue samples showed inflammation with no evidence of malignancy. So, as indicated, my next ERCP would be for stent removal. The date was set for June 29, 2017.

June 15, 2017: During late afternoon, I began experiencing severe pains that mimicked pancreatitis. Remember that I was very acquainted with pancreatitis. I placed a call to my primary physician and was told to go to emergency and have them assess my condition. Emergency medical staff stated that my bloodwork was normal, and there was no evidence of pancreatitis. I stayed with a very low fat, easy digestive diet the next day, and all seemed to return to normal. I did not take any of the prescribed pain medication.

June 29, 2017: I was relieved. Finally, the stents would come out, and I would be finished. There was a light at the end of the tunnel. I would go on my scuba diving vacation, and this would all be behind me. After the procedure, the doctor came to see my husband and me. He indicated that the ducts still had signs of clogging. After removing the stents, another balloon sweep was performed, more tissue samples were taken for biopsy, and new stents were placed. Needless to say, I was concerned that this would be an ongoing problem, and I began having my suspicions. I was assured that the stents would not interfere with my scuba diving plans. A few days after the procedure, I phoned the doctor's office and learned that the tissue samples were atypical but negative for cancer. It was explained to me that atypical cells can also be present from infection. My concerns were somewhat put to rest, but there was always that "red flag" in the back of my mind. Instinct is strong. My next ERCP for stent removal was scheduled for August 3, 2017.

I also recall having a conversation with the nurse from my GI doctor's office and questioning her as to how many times this procedure may need to be repeated before all was back to normal. I felt as though we were not making any forward progress and did not want to find that these procedures were going to be the "norm" in my life. She explained that the length of these treatments varied for each individual and that this procedure could correct the issue in one or two treatments or, as in some cases, could go on for quite some time, even as much as a few years. I was not comfortable with the prospect of having to do this every couple of months indefinitely.

July 20–30, 2017: St. Maarten was beautiful. We were so looking forward to enjoying time away from reality. The weather was perfect. One of our friends joined us, and the week really went well. I felt great, my energy level was good, and appetite was normal. I even did a few scuba dives. I was careful with what I chose to eat. Thursday evening, July 27, 2017, I experienced some indigestion. It was quite uncomfortable, but I took some antacid, and it seemed to subside. Friday morning, I felt great, so I didn't see any reason for concern. Cooking spices vary from island to island, so I attributed my indigestion to the change in cuisine.

July 30, 2017: We arrived at the St. Maarten airport for our return trip home. We grabbed a light lunch while waiting. We boarded our flight, got comfortable, and I began to read my book. The flight from St. Maarten to Charlotte, where we would board our connecting flight, was approximately four hours. About two hours into the flight, I began to feel ill. I nudged my husband to see if he had any antacid. He didn't, but we got some soda from the stewardess, and that seemed to calm down my abdominal discomfort. About fifteen minutes later, the pain returned and became excruciating, and the nausea was out of control. I asked my husband for an airline sick bag, and he got me two. I began vomiting uncontrollably. The young mom sitting next to my husband assumed that I was suffering from motion sickness. Fortunately, the airline staff didn't notice. We chose to say nothing because we were halfway between St. Maarten and Charlotte over the ocean. There would have been nowhere to land. The flight would have had to fly two hours and return to St. Maarten or continue on for two hours into Charlotte. Given my history, all I wanted was to return home to the States and my medical team.

We landed in Charlotte. Although I was no longer vomiting, the pain was so severe, and I began to have chills, most likely from the pain. I was extremely pale. A young man waiting for the same flight to Chicago as we were leant me his blanket, which I used for the entire flight. Our plane to Chicago was delayed by one and a half hours. I looked at my husband and told him I didn't think I could make it home. Of course, panic sets in because you are in an unfamiliar state without knowledge of the hospitals in the area and out of my insurance network. We were both concerned about my having to be hospitalized in Charlotte. But I toughed it out and made it to Chicago. We did not walk in the house until 2:00 a.m. Monday. I was exhausted, but the pain started to subside.

July 31, 2017: Four hours after arriving home from the airport, at 6:00 a.m., I woke up extremely ill and again in a great deal of pain. I elected not to take any pain medication. My husband called emergency services to transport me to the hospital. My body just wasn't willing to wait until August 3 for my regularly scheduled ERCP.

July 31–August 2, 2017: After completing the blood tests in the emergency room, the staff contacted my GI doctor, and he ordered that I be admitted. Again, my levels showed an issue with my digestive tract. A CT scan was also performed of my abdomen showing the biliary duct dilation, which, as noted earlier, could be due to chronic pancreatitis or primary sclerosing cholangitis. On Tuesday, August 1, 2017, the doctor performed another ERCP. A balloon sweep was done to again clear the debris from the bile ducts. Both stents were removed, and more tissue samples were taken for biopsy. A replacement stent was placed in my common bile duct; however, the stent in my hepatic duct was not replaced. It was decided that the tissue samples would be sent to Mayo Clinic for testing. The final report was issued by Mayo Clinic on August 9, 2017. Again, the biopsy revealed the cells were atypical but negative as to malignancy. As in the other tissue sample reports, a notation was made indicating that not all malignancies will present themselves in the tissue samples. It can be dependent upon the adequacy of the samples and the ability to detect tumor cells even when present. The recommendation was that I meet with the GI staff to further discuss my condition and to schedule a date to remove the common bile duct stent. We agreed to meet on September 11, 2017.

August 2017: A few weeks went by, and I seemed to be tolerating things well until the Thursday before Labor Day. I began experiencing nausea and severe pain. I called the GI doctor's office and left a message for his nurse. I stopped all food intake and waited to hear from the nurse. By Friday afternoon, my GI tract calmed down, and the pain subsided. I never did hear from the nurse, and since my appointment was just around the corner, I chose to do nothing and wait. No trips to the emergency room. Again, no pain medication was taken.

Prior to my meeting with the physician assistant, I had collaborated with two dear friends of mine, one of whom was very well versed in anatomy. Marla spent a great deal of time with me. She became my patient advocate, and I am forever grateful for her insight and direction. It proved to be very important in my meeting on September 11.

September 11, 2017: I met with the physician assistant, and the meeting started with a review of the various procedures, which had been performed and are outlined in this chapter. I listened carefully and patiently. I knew prior to the meeting that the only way to make your position heard is by remaining calm and collecting your thoughts. Otherwise, your emotions will take control, and you begin to sound more like a disgruntled patient rather than a patient on a mission. I had total faith and trust in my GI doctor and knew that he was as suspect and frustrated as I was.

Once the physician assistant completed her review, I requested that a thorough review of my records from the gallbladder removal be done. We discussed the comment by that physician about the small size of my duct. Maybe those records would show something that could assist in finding a solution to my current problem. I further indicated that although some people go through this process for a very long time without any improvement, that was not acceptable to me. At this point, I felt as though treating the symptoms took precedence over finding the underlying cause. Also, insurance companies have a great deal of control as to what procedures will be done and when. Since we need health insurance, the standard of care rendered by doctors is at the mercy of the insurance companies. Tests and procedures are approved based on the history of a majority of patients and the outcomes of their treatment protocol.

I point-blank asked if she could look me in the eye and confirm that I did not have pancreatic cancer. She answered, "No." I also inquired if there was any additional testing that we could do to facilitate identifying whether or not I had cancer. She ordered a CA19-9 blood test. Antigens are substances that cause our immune system to respond. CA19-9 is a type of antigen released by pancreatic cancer cells. She referred to it as a tumor marker. Not all pancreatic cancer patients have high CA19-9 levels, and there are some other conditions that can cause that marker to rise. You cannot confirm pancreatic cancer by a CA19-9 test, but it certainly was worth investigating. In addition, she suggested that we schedule the removal of the stent for October 2, 2017. They would again take tissue samples for biopsy. I was going to check the blood test results when I went for my next procedure in October.

September 19, 2017: Eight days after our meeting, I found myself in extreme pain and suffering from severe nausea. No, I did not take the pain medication. My husband drove me to the emergency room. An ultrasound was ordered, and the results showed that my pancreatic and biliary ducts were dilated. My GI doctor was contacted, and he gave the order to admit me in order to perform another ERPC, balloon sweep the ducts, and take ampullary tissue samples. Blood was drawn, and my lipase level had risen to 1,749

U/L. My common bile duct was now dilated to 16 mm. Food was withheld so that my pancreas could calm down. My CA19-9 was at 38 U/L. The normal range is 0–35 U/L.

September 21, 2017: The ERCP was performed, tissue samples were obtained, the old stent was removed, and a new one inserted. I remained in the hospital especially given the elevated lipase level.

September 24, 2017: The report of my tissue samples had been reviewed by the doctor, and one of the physician assistants came in and delivered the news. I had ampullary carcinoma. I was by myself in a cold hospital room. I called my husband and my girlfriend, Penny. I was crying hysterically. I did not even know what ampullary cancer was. I only knew that it was cancer, and that is the only word I heard.

Medical professionals have the unfortunate task of delivering devastating results to patients. It takes a certain amount of detachment to be able to perform this very important task. However, they should never lack empathy. I wish staff had contacted my family to have them there with me when I received the devastating news. No one should receive this type of news alone in a hospital room. Patients should have their family present when being delivered such results. The initial emotional and mental support is so important to the patient as they try to digest the possible death sentence they have just been given.

September 25, 2017: While still in the hospital, the surgeon met with me to introduce himself and share what the course of treatment would be for ampullary carcinoma. He provided a packet of information for my review regarding the procedure that would be performed and asked me to phone his office for an appointment so that we could meet prior to scheduling a surgery date. It was called a Whipple procedure and was the only course of treatment for this type of cancer. He also asked what I was feeling, and I responded that I felt I needed to go home and spend time with my family and with my dogs. He agreed.

I was kept in the hospital until September 27, 2017. Prior to discharge, a CT scan of my chest and abdomen showed the biliary stent, a dilated pancreatic duct, and bilateral lung nodules. My blood tests had somewhat returned to normal, and I was released. It was good to go home.

Be sure to set your boundaries with your medical team. I should have alerted the medical staff of the doctors' offices and the hospital that only when family is present with me should results be shared. Most times, you will have that internal warning system telling you that the results may not be what you want to hear. As we get older, that is more likely to be the case. Just make sure that the doctor and his staff, as well as the hospital staff, are well aware of the conditions under which you want to receive your results. Your support system will help you cope. You need them.

4

Whipple Surgery

Have you ever had to prepare for an event in your life that you were not familiar with? Maybe it was that first blind date. Or maybe it was your first home closing. You have no road map to guide you through the process, no how-to manual, and the only way to navigate and learn is by traveling the course. In the fall of 2017, I found myself in that exact situation.

As instructed by Dr. RG, my surgeon, I phoned and scheduled an appointment to meet with him. The meeting was set for the afternoon of October 9, 2017. I opened the packet of information he had given me regarding the procedure and shared it with my family. We all wrote down our questions for the meeting. This was a process each of us needed to do in our own privacy and space. It was extremely difficult for me, as the patient, and my family, as caregivers, to understand all that had been thrown at us. Now we had to make sense of all we were about to face.

Even after reading the booklet, which described the procedure in detail, I truly did not understand the gravity of this type of surgery. But I tried to step out of my life and approach the information from a detached position so that I could formulate questions. The details of the surgery seemed something out of a science fiction movie. I had certainly never heard of it and felt impatient and angry at having to review the material. I was reading words. I was not mentally ready to grasp all that was about to happen. Many times, I had to stop, breathe, and restart the review of materials. What I did learn from my review on the Internet is that if the doctor and hospital have performed several Whipple procedures, the fatality rate is about 20 percent. That does not account for setbacks from the surgery that require rehospitalization. If the doctor and hospital do not have several of these surgeries under their belt, then the fatality rate rises dramatically.

After about a week, I managed to type up a list of questions and reviewed them with my family. The list was as follows:

1. I have read that ampullary cancer is very rare and there is no real treatment protocol to gauge whether chemo and/or radiation will be effective. Will I need this follow-up treatment after surgery? Answer: I will need to consult with an oncologist, so I was advised to choose and meet with one prior to my surgery.

2. What are the chances of this type of cancer recurring within a five-year period? Answer: 80 percent chance of recurrence within the first two years, 20 percent chance of recurrence in years three to five, and the same chance as we all have of developing cancer after year five, roughly 10 percent.

3. Will removing the head of my pancreas affect the insulin levels in my body? Answer: No.

4. Am I having a portion of my stomach and/or a portion of my small intestine removed in addition to the head of my pancreas and common bile duct? Answer: Yes to all.

5. Am I correct in assuming that my surgery is not a distal pancreatectomy? Answer: Yes. My surgery was a pancreaticoduodenectomy, which is the common treatment for cancer in the head of the pancreas as well as for cancers found in the bile duct and duodenum (the first part of the small intestine). Note that the other type of procedure would involve removal of my total spleen and body/tail of the pancreas.

6. Is the decision to use Jackson-Pratt drains standard operating procedure, and would I be coming home with those drains still in place? Answer: Yes, that is standard operating procedure, and a determination would be made before my release from the hospital as to whether or not those drains could be removed. It would be dependent upon my body's ability to absorb excess fluid that occurs after a surgery of this kind.

7. Do I come home with an anesthesia pump? Answer: No. A pain medication prescription would be provided so that I could manage my discomfort by taking the medication orally.

8. The head of the pancreas manufactures most of the digestive enzymes our body needs for the breakdown of food. I understand I will be placed on oral enzymes. Is this a medication I will have to take for the rest of my life? Answer: Most likely, yes.

9. How long would recovery take? Answer: Six weeks to regain 50 percent of your strength, and twelve weeks to regain 100 percent, if you work at it. Recovery time sounded reasonable to me.

10. I have stairs at home. Will this be an issue? Answer: No. I could use the stairs as an exercise to encourage recovery.

As intelligent as I felt my questions were, I was absolutely still very much in denial. In fact, at one point, I looked at the surgeon who had a great sense of humor and stated: "I have things to do, places to go, and people to see. I have already lined up substitute instructors for my fitness classes. Let's get this going in the next couple of days so that I can get back to my life." Even with his sense of humor, the surgeon gave me an unusual look. Of course, it wouldn't be long before I understood why. His physician assistant, Jen, merely explained that there was a scheduling process in place, and so it couldn't happen that quickly. She left the room while we continued to chat with the surgeon and returned shortly to let us know my surgery would be the afternoon of October 24, 2017. Two more weeks to wait. It's just natural to fear that as each day passes, the cancer grows that much more. Impatience becomes a temporary new normal.

One item that requires noting is during our meeting, the surgeon shared that when a woman in her sixties develops gallbladder issues, that raises a red flag for him. As I understood him, younger people are more unkind to themselves with their eating habits, and sometimes there are weight issues, as well as other factors. Many times, fast food is a steady part of their diet. As such, it is more likely for the gallbladder to go bad. By age sixty, we treat ourselves better and have hopefully acquired healthier eating habits. The chance of a gallbladder going bad is greatly reduced. So here we are. I can't help but think my gallbladder was the first sign of the cancer that was hiding in my ampulla. It is also important to note that I don't feel anything would have changed if this would have been flagged when the doctor discovered the small opening during my gallbladder operation. Most likely, standard procedure would have been to monitor my health with periodic testing. But if it had been flagged, maybe something from that hospital record would have alerted the GI doctor to create a different plan that would include blood tests that would monitor cancer tumor markers. I cannot help but wonder.

Prior to leaving the surgeon's office, PA Jen gave me a list of items I needed to purchase to physically prepare for surgery. The items included supplements, probiotics, and a special cleanser. There were also cardio exercises to do, which would enhance my stamina in preparation for surgery and recovery. As we wrapped up the meeting, I remember Dr. RG saying to me, "If you have any other questions, please call. In the meantime, get your affairs in order." Again, being in denial, I explained to everyone that he just wanted me to make sure that my responsibilities in running the house were addressed and covered. I was not willing to look at it any other way. He also warned me to expect a weight loss of about 20 percent. I was 134 pounds going into the surgery. A 20 percent weight loss would put me at five feet, eight inches tall and a weight of approximately 108 pounds.

My goal was to be able to share my ongoing information and surgery updates with several individuals. In order to make it easier for my husband, I created a group contact list so that my husband could easily create and send e-mails with updates from my surgery and recovery. This avoided having to respond individually to people and reduced the number of phone calls. In addition, it was a great way to memorialize my entire surgery and treatment in the event issues arose or if there were any questions as to the standard of care I was receiving. I did the same thing when my mother was sick the last several months of her life. Having realized then that it was a great way to track the health care her doctors and the hospital were providing, I felt it would serve me well to do the same.

My second order of business was to find an oncologist that was in my HMO insurance network and set up an appointment as quickly as possible. I worked with my primary doctor and found an individual who resonated with me. I met with her, and she was wonderful. I felt confident after meeting with her as she took a careful look at my history and was ready to move forward after my surgery with a definite plan. She was confident, and I liked that. As I already knew and she confirmed, there was no treatment protocol for this type of cancer, so she would follow the treatment suggested by the medical industry for post-Whipple patients. She suspected that I would undergo six months of chemotherapy. She also explained that there were several chemotherapy options if I found that I wanted to change the prescribed chemo drug based on the severity of the symptoms I was enduring.

I was in charge of all household finances, so my third order of business was to be sure that all of our household expenses were accounted for and all monthly bills set up on automatic payment. I also prepared a list for my husband, so if any questions arose regarding household expenses, he could refer to the list and get the answers he needed.

My last order of business was to research the Internet to get a better understanding of ampullary carcinoma and Whipple surgery. Wow! There were only a few sites that addressed ampullary carcinoma and one study conducted several years ago.

An article published by the International Hepato-Pancreato-Biliary Association[1] indicates that,

> Ampullary malignancies are rare tumors with a reported incidence of fewer than one case per 100,000 population... The incidence of ampullary malignancy increases with advancing age, most notably after the age of 50 years...the median age at diagnosis is 65 years.

I was sixty-four years old when diagnosed. In another article published by the National Center for Biotechnology Information,[2] it is written that "[t]he cancer of the ampulla is a rare disease with an incidence of less than one per 100,00." The article further states "that woman are found to be less frequently affected (0.36/100000) than men (0.56/1000000). [A]verage age at diagnosis is between 60 and 70."

I also learned that the American Cancer Society lists ampullary carcinoma as a subcategory under pancreatic cancer. I wondered then, and still do now, how long before the cancer would have spread to my pancreas and liver had it not been caught early. Thankfully, I'll never know.

In the two weeks prior to surgery, I prepared for the surgery in accordance with the instructions from the surgeon. I became very anxious the last few days. I just wanted all this behind me.

On the day of surgery, we arrived at the hospital at 1:30 p.m. I was taken to a temporary room so that they could get me into surgical dress and start my IV drip. All procedures were on schedule, and my surgery was to begin at 2:30. Ten minutes before surgery, the surgeon came to see me and was very upbeat with his great sense of

---

[1] James Askew and Saxon Connor, "Review of the Investigation and surgical management of resectable ampullary adenocarcinoma," International Hepato-Pancreato-Biliary Association, 2013.

[2] Francesca Panzeri, Stefano Crippa, and Massimo Falconi, "Management of ampullary neoplasms: A tailored approach between endoscopy and surgery," National Center for Biotechnology Information, May 4, 2015.

humor. I know he was trying to lessen my angst, but it really did not work. I remember telling him that he needed to have a slice of pizza ready for me to eat after surgery. I was starving. He replied, "There are two things I can tell you with certainty. You won't want that piece of pizza after surgery, and you are going to hate me." He left, and as they wheeled me down to surgery, the nurses wished me well. I let them know in no uncertain terms that "Death is not an option. I am going to beat this!" Off I went.

Approximately six hours later, my surgery was finished, and my family notified that I had done well. It took a couple of hours to waken from the anesthetic. All I remember is family and friends kissing me and a lot of pain. And yes, the doctor was right. I did not want that slice of pizza or any food for that matter, and I did hate him. The pain was off the charts.

I remember waking up in my room and the nurses asking me several questions regarding my pain level and any other issues I was experiencing. I was given additional medication and fell back to sleep. The next morning, I woke, and it pained me to breathe. Later that first day, PA Jen came in to check on me, and I said to her, "I wish you had let me die on that table." I cried. She tried her best to console me. So there I laid, in a great deal of pain, with a feeding tube on the left side of my stomach and two drain tubes on the right side of my stomach. Every couple of hours, the CNA would empty the bags attached to my drain tubes and change the dressings on my drain tubes and feeding tube. This must be a nightmare I was living. This isn't what I imagined, and this is not the way I wanted it to work. This was a deviation from my plans.

A few days after surgery, the surgeon ordered therapy to get me walking and moving. As I sat up in preparation for the therapist, I remember feeling somewhat in a fog and mentioned this to the nurse. Seconds later, I had passed out. It took about ten seconds for me to regain consciousness. Therapy came but decided to put my session on hold. The nurse immediately ordered a blood test. My blood counts were very low, most likely from the bleeding associated with the surgery. I was administered two units of blood.

Each day, the surgeon and PA would visit to check on my progress. The day after receiving the units of blood, I was able to get out of bed with assistance and use the restroom. A therapy session was held, and I was able to walk a short distance with a walker. That was progress for me! I was told that the surgeon removed the head of my pancreas, my common bile duct, the twelve lymph nodes surrounding my bile duct, a part of my small intestine, and a part of my stomach. The staging of my tumor was T3 N0 M0. *T3* tumor staging is based on size. My tumor was 2.3 cm. *N0* meant no cancer in the nearby nodes, and *M0* meant there was no metastasis. This is called the TNM staging and is probably the most common used. Because some lymph nodes were removed, there was also a chance of my developing lymphedema in my abdomen. Fortunately, that did not happen; although, I understand lymphedema can present itself at any time, even years down the road.

As my blood test results improved and I was tolerating a liquid GI diet, it was determined that I should be discharged to continue my recovery at home. There was no point in keeping me as there is a great deal of exposure to viruses and infections in the hospital. It was also decided that my drain tubes would be removed, but I would go home with a feeding tube. Having some of the tubes removed was a relief. Having tubes feels so unnatural. After removal and shortly before receiving my discharge documents, a nutritionist came in to see me to discuss my nutritional needs for life after Whipple. I was released November 1, 2017, which was the one-year anniversary of my gallbladder surgery!

Life After Whipple

How do you prepare for a new normal or can you? How do you prepare for a whole new reality? Like going on that first blind date, you have no road map to guide you. I understood that I would have to make some dietary changes, but my new normal was not what I was expecting. It was not even a close call!

A couple of days prior to being discharged, a social worker at the hospital met with my husband and me to discuss my needs once home. It was determined that I would need a hospital bed, a pole to hang the supplemental nutrition bags, the nutrition supplement, and wound dressings. All items were ordered, delivered, and set up the day before I was released. A referral order had also been submitted to have a nurse visit twice a week to check on my progress and assist my husband with any issues he had as to the wound cleansing, bandage changing, and feeding tube maintenance. Even though the nurses at the hospital gave my husband a couple of lessons on his responsibilities, these tasks can be overwhelming, and there is no way to anticipate what problems might arise.

I arrived home on Wednesday and by Saturday, November 4, 2017. I woke up in the morning with severe abdominal pain. I convinced myself that if I could somehow get out of bed and walk a little, the pain would go away. It did not, and my husband heard me crying as I laid on the floor. My family contacted emergency services, and I was transported back to the hospital. I felt so hopeless and defeated.

Given the recent Whipple procedure, I was admitted. My blood test showed a high white blood cell count, platelet count, and neutron absolute. An infection was suspected. A CT scan was also done, and the results showed a high collection of fluid in the abdomen, which was pressing on all the organs that had just been surgically altered and connected. The fluid was either blood products from hemorrhaging during the surgery or postoperative pancreatic fluid, the latter which is not uncommon. Dr. RG gave the order to admit me so that my postoperative issues could be addressed. Tube feedings were stopped until the condition could be corrected.

I was placed on an IV of antibiotics and pain medication, as well as fluids to keep me hydrated. Over the next couple of days, I was stabilized. A discussion was had with Dr. RG and the hospital staff, and the decision was made to have intervention radiology reinsert drainage tubes so that the excess fluid could drain and samples be collected for testing. The procedure was performed on November 6, 2017, and 100 cc of fluid was removed and sent for cultures. I also developed severe diarrhea and abdominal cramping. I was administered additional medication to reduce the cramping and aid in returning to normal bowel function. We now had to wait for the results from the cultures.

It was determined that there was no hemorrhaging, and the fluid appeared to be nothing more than pancreatic fluid. Postoperative fluid is generally absorbed by the body; however, my body was unable to do so. Tube feedings were resumed, and I was monitored to be sure that all my blood counts returned to normal. My intestinal cramping was being controlled with medication, and bowel function had improved. On November 10, all issues having been addressed and somewhat resolved, I was discharged from the hospital to continue my in-home recovery. My mobility had suffered from the lengthy hospital stays, and I was extremely weak. The road to recovery would be long, and I was depressed.

The next new normal was learning how to eat. Most important is you should not eat anything that is going to cause you to vomit or experience dry heaves. The reason is that this type of jerking motion on your body can undo the stitches used to reconnect what is left of your digestive system. Also, one of the side effects of Whipple surgery is the dumping syndrome. Dumping syndrome is a term used to describe a group of symptoms that occur when the stomach empties too quickly. These symptoms can occur ten minutes to three hours after eating. As you recall, the head of my pancreas that produces digestive enzymes was removed, I had no gallbladder which is a storehouse for digestive enzymes, a part of my stomach was removed, which is where food begins the digestion process, and a part of my small intestine had been removed, which is where important nutrients are absorbed. My digestion system had been redesigned and needed to function with fewer parts. My body needed time to adjust to the new anatomy, which can take up to a year or even longer. In the interim, your diet consists of low fats, low carbs, no sugar, and small meals. Instead of the usual three healthy meals, you are now reduced to six small meals with snacks in between the meals. I also needed to gain weight, but how do you do that when you eliminate carbs and sugar? Even with the new diet, I was still experiencing the dumping syndrome. Because of this syndrome, I lost almost 20 percent of my body weight, which is what I expected. My husband recalls my weigh-in at the doctor's office about three weeks after surgery to be 112 pounds. At five feet, eight inches tall, I looked and probably was somewhat malnourished. I also needed to go on vitamin supplements since a part of my small intestine had been removed, and this is where the very important task of nutrients is extracted to help maintain your life, especially iron. To date, the vitamin supplements are working, but it is not uncommon for Whipple patients, five or six years post-surgery, to need iron infusions. I don't know if that will be in my future, a possible new twist in my roller-coaster ride.

Each day I watched my husband prepare wonderful meals, and all I could eat were three or four small bites. The nausea would start, and the food no longer appealed to me. I knew that if I became truly malnourished, I would be hospitalized. I could think of many places I would love to be, but the hospital was not one of them. To supplement what little I ate, each night my husband hooked up a bag of nutrition to my feeding tube. In addition, I tried to drink two bottles of a nutritional supplement each day that were high in calories. Unfortunately, I was only able to drink one because of the fat content. I knew I was a long way from finding my "new normal."

As the holidays approached, I found myself becoming more and more depressed. I refused to speak with anyone and gave strict instructions to my family not to allow any visitors. The excuses I had were believable and acceptable. Thankfully, I think most of my friends and family knew I needed to find my inner peace, and they honored that. I rarely got out of bed, and a friend of ours gave me a cow bell to ring in the event I needed assistance from my family. It was obvious that the depression deepened, and I began to use the bell for simple things, such as needing a drink of water. After a few days, my husband hid the cowbell, which forced me to work on my mobility. One of the gifts a caregiver needs is to be able to determine when assistance should be given and when it shouldn't. This is crucial to recovery.

On December 12, 2017, I met with my surgeon to discuss my progress and the meeting with the oncologist. My appetite improved and so did my weight. The excess fluid seemed to resolve itself, and I was eating a bit more, so the feeding and drain tubes were removed. I am free at last. I was looking forward to enjoying my Christmas dinner and the holidays. It felt great having a somewhat normal appetite. This was a sign of progress. Even my weight showed some improvement. I did have to order a couple of pairs of pants and tops in a smaller size as everything I had was too big.

It took eighteen months after surgery to find my "new normal." I will always have to monitor and balance my food choices each day and determine the amount of digestive enzymes needed for each meal. I am careful with my food choices when traveling. Not doing so is a sure way to ruin a perfectly good vacation. I can safely say that, as of this writing, I am back to eating 80 percent of the foods I used to eat. However, each day continues to be a learning experience, and I do have to keep balancing my food choices.

Always ask questions regarding what setbacks from surgery you might encounter. You also want to understand what effects carbohydrates, fats, and sugars have on your digestive system so that you can slowly and safely introduce new food groups to your digestive system. There are no shortcuts, and ignoring your body's response to different foods is dangerous.

Chemotherapy, Counseling, Medical Marijuana

All the prongs of this new "normal" had to be discovered, sorted, and accommodated into my life. So much had come to pass, so many things had changed, and yet I still had to go on and press forward. Just when you think you have somewhat mastered these new changes, nothing is as it seems.

Prior to my December visit with my surgeon, I met with the oncologist on November 17, 2017, for my postoperative assessment. We discussed my overall health, and she shared the accepted form of treatment for my situation. We also discussed my mental state.

I think it is very important to note here that I did not share the depth of my depression with the oncologist. When asked, I made a comment in passing about feeling a "little down" once in a while. She explained that what I was feeling was normal. After all, I just suffered from a catastrophic illness and surgery, so I was entitled to have a pity party now and then. I was uncomfortable and embarrassed to suggest that I was suffering from severe depression. There is a stigma associated with depression. I did not want to be judged. It is unfortunate that even in today's day and age, depression is still negatively viewed. In the years prior to my diagnosis, I was equally guilty of frowning on individuals who suffered from depression. It is a misunderstood illness. The truth was that I was severely depressed and, as I later learned, suffering from post-traumatic stress disorder. My anxiety before each test result and doctor's visit was extreme. Sadly, I was more concerned about having judgment passed on me than getting the treatment I needed. For all those suffering from depression, I understand it; I get it. I can only speak as to cancer as that is what I know. The standard operating procedure for medical teams treating cancer patients should include treatment by a mental health professional. A positive attitude is paramount to fighting this disease as well as aiding in recovery.

My oncologist explained that we had several chemotherapy options available since there was no protocol as to treatment. If I was unable to tolerate one chemotherapy, there would be other chemotherapy options. There were also several medications that could be prescribed to help offset the nausea and vomiting induced by the treatment. The chemotherapy we agreed on was capecitabine and available in pill form. I would take it orally for two weeks, have one week off, and repeat the process. It would be a course of treatment over a six-month period. Sounded easy and doable to me.

The next item to be addressed was the start date of chemo. The general rule is chemo begin no later than sixty days post-surgery. Since my surgery was October 24, that would mean my start date was to be December 24, Christmas Eve. I explained to the oncologist that in 2016, gallbladder removal interfered with my ability to enjoy the holiday season and meals. The holidays are important to me and my family. I had recently been diagnosed with a rare cancer and underwent surgery that could have been fatal. Christmas was, personally, a very important holiday for me. I was not going to give up enjoying the holiday because of chemotherapy. After all, I had no idea what my future held, and I wanted quality time and an opportunity to make memories with my family over the holiday season. She saw no harm in delaying the start of chemo to December 26, 2017.

As Christmas approached, I had a great deal of fear that since my mother passed on Christmas Day, was that going to be my fate? My husband tried to console me but to no avail. Just another indication of how important therapy is. This is definitely the post-traumatic stress disorder rearing its ugly head.

As agreed, I began taking the chemo tablets December 26. The first two weeks of treatment went very well. I had some nausea, but the medication prescribed seemed to help. I never realized that chemo has a cumulative effect. A couple of days into my second round, I experienced severe nausea. It was crippling. I couldn't eat, I was exhausted, and the anti-nausea medications prescribed were depressants, and so I fell deeper into my depression. Thankfully, this was the trigger that forced me to hit bottom and acknowledge that I needed help. Besides, how could I return to teaching my classes and promote the benefits of staying active when I was not even following my own rules. I was absolutely terrified that my inability to get moving would get back to my classes, and they would lose all faith in me. My first order of business was to contact my oncologist to change my chemo, and the second was to call my insurance and find an approved therapist in my network. I got an emergency visit with my doctor and found a therapist who was able to see me immediately.

Gemczar was the new chemotherapy treatment prescribed. It would have to be delivered intravenously, and it was suggested I consider having a port placed since I had five more months of treatment to complete as well as weekly blood draws. This chemotherapy would be administered once per week for three weeks, followed by a one-week rest. I thought a great deal about the port and decided against it. The site of the port is an open area and prone to infections. I was not willing to risk developing another medical issue. The normal range of blood counts for chemotherapy patients is lower than the range of healthy individuals. That also means that the ability to fight viruses and infections is more difficult. I knew my veins were already tired from the countless hospital visits and surgery, but I wanted to avoid the port.

Prior to starting this new chemo treatment, the therapist met with me and issued her assessment. I was not only battling depression but also had post-traumatic stress disorder. I needed to learn how to manage both conditions and to accept that the PTSD was with me for life. And so, more appointments and doctors on the schedule. I also recognized that my depression also deepened as St. Jude's Children's Hospital was running a large number of ads on television for donations during the holiday season. It caused me to question what right I had to expect to live through all this when children were suffering from this unforgiving disease. But that is for God to decide. Needless to say, a great deal of guilt accompanied my depression. The upside was that my husband and I became monthly donors to St. Jude's.

I was in therapy for a total of fifteen months. It was difficult to face my diagnoses. What I have come to learn is that a therapist should be a part of a cancer patient's treatment team. No one jumps for joy at being given the news that they have cancer. When I received my first cancer diagnosis in the hospital, I did not have to ask for or find a surgeon. He had come in to visit with me within twenty-four hours after being given the news. A therapist should also be assigned immediately as my mental state played an integral part in my healing. The fact is that it is up to our various specialty doctors to ask routine questions about your mental health, and this approach is so archaic and not beneficial. Because of the stigma attached to depression, no one wants to admit they desperately need help.

When I arrived for my first chemotherapy treatment, a nurse from my oncologist's office walked me back to a large room that had approximately ten recliners with chairs available for family members. There were snacks, water, coffee, and a bright and friendly nursing staff. We set up my monthly schedule, and the staff answered any questions. Before being administered the chemo, I was given an infusion of a steroid combined with Zofran for nausea. Once finished, the chemo treatment began.

The side effects from Gemczar are known to be less severe. Few individuals suffer hair loss, and many are able to tolerate the nausea. However, when the chemo is being administered, it does feel as if your vein is on fire. I never lost my hair; however, the nausea was difficult for the first three or four days after treatment. As for the burning sensation, the nurses would provide an ice pack to place on the area, and they would slow the IV drip. I was able to tolerate it. The nurses were always attentive and made sure you were as comfortable as possible. Sometimes I would read a book or my husband and I would watch TV, which was available in the treatment area. I am not sure what was more devastating to me, being diagnosed with cancer or watching poison being fed through my veins.

To add a little levity to the situation that seemed so grave, I received the chemo treatments, but my husband lost clumps of hair. I remember looking at my husband one day during my chemo treatment, and he had one eyebrow totally missing. As he got up to get me something to drink, I noticed bald spots on the back of his head that he never had. That was the first moment that I realized all the stress he was experiencing and trying to cope with. I offered if he wanted therapy, but he said he didn't. He felt the hair would come back once I was found to have no evidence of the disease. And yes, that did happen. But just an indication how stressful the situation can be for your caregivers. They will generally suffer in silence so as not to place an additional burden on you. Watch for the signs of the stress placed on your caregivers. If they become ill, they can't help you, and you can't help them.

As a chemotherapy patient, you are warned to avoid sun and to drink plenty of fluids. There were a couple of instances where I had developed a fever and suffered from exhaustion. I would call the office, and they would have me come in immediately to receive an IV of fluids. I was dehydrated. After receiving the fluids, my whole being changed. The fever was gone, and my energy level improved. It is so important to keep yourself hydrated during chemotherapy.

Early into my chemotherapy, my therapist had reviewed the list of anti-nausea medications and advised that because they were depressants, I needed to speak with the doctor about stopping the use of them for nausea. That was when I realized that I needed to educate myself better on the various medications I had been prescribed. Although I did stop the medications, the nausea still needed to be addressed. Illinois had just recently legalized medical marijuana. Because this was such a new approach to medical treatment, the doctor's office knew very little about the application process. Their knowledge was limited to the form they needed to complete to certify my condition for the medical marijuana license that was mailed under separate cover to the state. The doctor certifies your condition, and the patient, as licensee, completes and submits their own application.

After researching the State of Illinois site, I downloaded and printed all the necessary forms and completed them. I obtained a photo for my license as required by the state and selected a company approved by the state for fingerprinting purposes. Once submitted, the process takes approximately three months. However, there were a couple of glitches in my application. The doctor's office had completed the wrong form, so I contacted them to complete and mail the correct form. In addition, there weren't enough recognizable points on my fingerprints. I contacted the company, and they prepared a letter to the state indicating that chemo patients generally lose their fingerprints, so there would be no point in repeating the process. I mailed the company's letter back to the state with the documents. Shortly after, I received correspondence from the state requesting that I submit additional funds so that the state police could run a background check. I complied, and these delays added another month to the process. I applied for a two-year license since I didn't know what my future held.

Once I received my license, I was able to begin a better treatment over my nausea. Since it is not a legalized prescription drug, out-of-pocket costs are very high. My only regret was not doing more research on the different varieties of medical marijuana available and which strains would effectively treat my symptoms. The staff at the medical marijuana facility were not overly helpful, but when I applied for my license, this facility was the one I listed on my application as it was close to home. It took about two months to find that right combination of marijuana. Even when licensed, the use of medical marijuana is restricted to your home. You cannot travel with it. It does not matter what your mode of transportation is. So you do need to keep approved medications on hand for those times when you are out and about or traveling.

There will be those individuals, be it family, friends, or acquaintances, who will have negative things to say about your use of marijuana to control the symptoms. Sometimes, those who are not supportive can even be downright cruel. Just remember, it is easy for them to pass judgment when they walk in healthy shoes. Do what you need to do for yourself, and distance yourself from these individuals. They do not have your best interest at heart.

With therapy and chemo well underway, I really felt I had turned a corner. Admittedly, my stamina was not 100 percent, but I was headed in the right direction. In early 2017, I had made two commitments. The first was to take my sister on a Caribbean cruise. Deposits had been paid, and we were to set sail in early April 2018. The second commitment was to my dear friend, Penny. We had submitted our deposits to go on a hiking and kayaking adventure in early May 2018. I have always been a person who takes commitment very seriously, and these were no exceptions. In spite of being on chemo, I was going to enjoy myself. There is a sense of urgency that develops when you experience a catastrophic illness or surgery. There is the realization that once gone, all that is left of your life are memories and photos. As long as I was able, I was not going to miss making those memories and taking those photos. My oncologist was superb, and we scheduled chemo around my vacation plans. Careful eating and proper rest would ensure a great trip.

The oncology nursing staff was wonderful. As my trips neared, I shared my plans with them. They were extremely concerned about all I had planned while still on chemotherapy and approached my oncologist with their concerns. She put their fears at rest and explained that I was merely making my memories. The chemo schedule was modified, and necessary blood tests would be taken so that any issues could be addressed prior to my vacations. It was so nice to learn that they paid attention to what was happening in their patients' lives and addressed the concerns they had. These nurses had such a passion for their work. I admired them and felt blessed.

In March, I went back to work teaching my aqua aerobics classes. Many people asked how I was able to do that while on chemotherapy. Simply put, I did not know I couldn't do it. If you believe, then you can do it! Tinley Fitness was the first facility I worked at, and they were so kind to have a veteran instructor with me as I taught my first class to be sure I was ready to undertake teaching. She was there to step in if I felt I didn't have the stamina to finish the class. She was with me for as many classes as I needed her to be there. Thank you to the instructor and my manager. It meant so much to me. After that first class, I was on my way! I then returned to Orland Park Health & Fitness. They also were so welcoming, and my manager was so kind. I probably went back to teaching way too soon. There was still four more months of treatments. But I needed strength to fight on this journey, and I found my strength through normalcy and activity. And teaching classes was my normal. This is also when and where I learned what it meant to be in the present. When I started teaching that first aqua aerobics class and felt the energy and excitement from the participants, it was so exhilarating, and I was so focused. I truly forgot about the fact that I was on chemo and feeling really tired. You cannot see or touch energy, but you can certainly feel it. And it does make you feel upbeat and alive. I lived in the moment of teaching that class, and for that hour, nothing else mattered.

The Caribbean cruise with my sister went extremely well. My digestive issues were kept to a minimum, and I made sure to get plenty of rest between ports. We had a fabulous time, and many great memories were made. It was so very special to enjoy this time with my sister. Again, always create memories and enjoy each moment to the fullest.

Prior to my hiking and kayaking trip with Penny, the oncologist suggested that I have an ERCP to check my digestive system and obtain tissue samples for biopsy. She contacted my GI doctor, and the procedure was scheduled for Tuesday, May 1, 2018. The results from that procedure would be available about a week thereafter. Our trip departure date was Saturday, May 5, 2018. The procedure was performed without incident, and a tissue sample was collected for testing. Midway into my trip, I phoned the doctor's office for the results, and all was normal. I felt as though I had been holding my breath since the day of the procedure. It felt wonderful to finally exhale. Life is good! The recommendation was that a follow-up ERCP be performed in a couple of months.

The San Juan Islands were beautiful, and we loved the hiking and kayaking. There were three levels of activities—easy, medium, and difficult. We chose the medium level of activity, and it worked perfectly. It takes being one with nature to experience all of God and get back in touch with your soul. I considered this trip being one with nature and God as my cancer-healing yoga. It works! When I first was diagnosed, Penny said to me, "I am with you." And she was, even through this trip and beyond. It was wonderful!

Teaching for the first time two months after starting chemotherapy and four months following my Whipple surgery.

Enjoying one of the ports during the cruise with my sister.

Just returned from kayaking during my hiking and kayaking
trip in the San Juan Islands with my dear friend Penny.

Biking a charity event seven weeks after I finished chemotherapy.

At the end of June, I finished my chemotherapy treatments,
and the third week of July, I left with our group to enjoy a wonderful scuba diving vacation on Bonaire. I held up well, and my dive
buddies were so supportive as they helped me with all my equipment in and out of the water. I cannot thank them enough. It felt so

wonderful to be under the water in a world that is so beautiful and mystifying. Again, my healing yoga and connecting with very special individuals that I share such a deep friendship with.

In August 2018, it was time to have the follow-up ERCP as well as a PET scan. The GI doctor scheduled my procedure for August 18, 2018, which ironically is my sister's birthday. I found this to be a good omen. The results of the ERCP and tissue biopsy were normal and negative for malignancy.

As you recall, a CT scan performed during my last hospital stay prior to Whipple surgery revealed nodules on both of my lungs. Since I was due for a scan, my oncologist ordered a PET scan that would cover the area from my neck to my hips. There is always a concern that not all cancer cells have been eradicated, so it is good procedure to run a scan of the entire area. My oncologist chose a PET scan. It is important to note that CT scans measure tumor growth and PET scans light up suspected cancer cells or problem areas. Not all cells that light up are cancerous. Infections can also cause the same result, and lymph nodes are storehouses for infections and immune disorders. But it is also true that benign nodules can turn cancerous.

My simple understanding of PET scan results is there is an illumination scale used to measure problem areas. Readings that illuminate 3.0 or under are areas to be monitored. Any areas that illuminate greater than 3.0 are cause for great concern and should be investigated. The more complex explanation as I understand it is there is a radioactive tracer that is attached to the glucose molecules injected into you prior to your scan. These molecules attach and light up any fast-dividing or fast-moving cells. Cancer cells are fast-producing, and the programmed death of these cells has been altered, which is why the disease takes over. It should be remembered that there are other reasons for cells to light up, such as infection, cardiovascular disease, pulmonary embolisms, etc. Radiologists know what to look for.

My recollection is that the lung nodules existed for quite some time and had appeared on several previous scans. I vaguely recall that there had been no change in size. When the PET scan results were released to my oncologist, the nodule on my right lung reached 6.8

on the illumination scale. The left lung was only at 1.6. My oncologist referred me to a pulmonologist to have an EBUS procedure at which time tissue samples could be removed for biopsy from the right lung. An EBUS is an endobronchial ultrasound that is considered minimally invasive but highly effective in securing tissue samples and diagnosing lung cancer.

Leave no stone unturned. Remember that early intervention is the key. When something abnormal appears on a scan, make sure it is investigated. Trust your gut instinct. Most times, it is your only early warning signal.

Right Lung Cancer and Radiation Treatment

W e all remember those roller-coaster rides we went on when we were younger. There are the ups and downs, the times when the speed accelerates beyond what we imagine, the sections where you slow down, and all the surprises along the way. All during the ride, you hope and pray to make it safely to the finish line. That's the thrill of a roller-coaster ride. Unfortunately, my right lung was going to put me on a roller-coaster ride that was anything but thrilling.

On October 2, 2018, the EBUS procedure was performed. An EBUS, as stated earlier, is an endoscopic ultrasound of the lung along with the ability to collect a tissue sample. It is an outpatient procedure, and the entire process from arrival to discharge took about three hours. The pulmonologist came to see me and advised me to contact his office for an appointment for the following week to receive the results. The following week, my husband and I met with the doctor, and he advised us that I did in fact have adenocarcinoma in the right lung; the good news is it was primary. This meant that it was not a metastasis from the original ampullary carcinoma but was a new cancer originating in the right lung. This disease certainly loves making a home in my body. He further recommended I needed to consult with a thoracic surgeon to discuss my treatment options.

The pulmonologist was leaning toward a lung lobectomy. The tumor was located between my middle and lower lobes, so the surgical option would be to remove those lobes leaving me with only one-third of my right lung intact. For information purposes, the right lung has three lobes and the left lung has two lobes. I was extremely apprehensive about this course of treatment and had great concerns about my ability to continue to bike ride, scuba dive, and teach fitness classes after such a procedure. I found the treatment recommendation to be alarming and was not comfortable with his indication that two-thirds of my right lung would more than likely have to be removed. I already had several body parts removed and was not anxious to undergo this surgery. My bigger concern was that if this drastic action was taken and the cancer could not be removed or if removed and then returned, where would I go from here?

It took about two weeks to obtain the insurance referral and secure an appointment with the thoracic surgeon. In the interim, I had an appointment with my chemo oncologist, and she shared some treatment options that I could at least investigate in preparation for my meeting with the surgeon. I returned home, got my pen and paper, and after doing some research, jotted down all my questions.

We met with the thoracic surgeon, and he was very thorough in explaining the location of the tumor and what that meant from a surgical standpoint. I asked him about other options and explained that I would prefer to avoid the surgery so long as it did not compromise my ability to fight the cancer in the future if a less invasive treatment option proved to be unsuccessful.

The first approach I explored with him was the process by which the genes involved could be identified and then target those genes with a very specific chemotherapy. He explained that this option was for individuals where standard treatments did not work. The second approach was cyber knife treatment, which is a specific application of radiation that targets the tumor only. The third option was the surgery.

He felt that given my overall health and fitness and given the size of the tumor, I would be an excellent candidate for the cyber knife radiation treatment. That being said, he recommended a radiation oncologist and provided the contact information. My medical team was growing in leaps and bounds. I obtained the required referral and within three weeks met with the radiation oncologist. Because he was in the network, he had access to my medical history. I was relieved to learn that I could have a better option than surgery.

We met with Dr. FV, the radiation oncologist, and after reviewing my history, we discussed my lung tumor. The staging of this lung tumor was T1b N0 M0. The pulmonologist originally told me that my lung tumor was stage 3. However, that was changed to my advantage. This staging meant that the tumor was larger than 5 mm but less than 10 mm. There was no lymph node involvement and no metastasis. The treatment recommended was SABR treatment, which was comparable to cyber knife. SABR treatment is also known as stereotactic ablative radiation treatment and is a highly focused radiation that gives an intense dose of radiation concentrating only on the tumor while limiting the dose to the surrounding organs. It also measures your breathing habits and adjusts the delivery of the radiation accordingly to keep it concentrated on the tumor only. The oncologist also felt I was a great candidate for this procedure, and he set the process in motion. He would review my biopsy results again but felt that I would not need more than five treatments. Dr. FV also shared that based on a discussion he had with the thoracic surgeon, they agreed to carefully watch the nodule in my left lung. I agreed. Remember, the nodule in my left lung only lit up to 1.6.

It took about three weeks to start the treatments. I was approved to receive up to 1,100 RADS per treatment session, per day. The first session was a "dry run" at which time all the markings were transferred to my torso. The risk was that the tumor was very near to my pulmonary artery, so the calculations had to be spot on. There was no room for error. Once that was completed and reviewed by the doctor, approval was given. I started treatments two days later. Unlike chemotherapy, I felt a little tired from the radiation but otherwise functioned normally. I would teach my aqua aerobics in the morning and follow it up with the radiation treatment. It worked well, and I was pleased. It was even more exciting to be finished after only five treatments.

A follow-up appointment was had, and we discussed the timing of my next CT scan and what I could expect. He also questioned whether or not I felt any ill effects from the radiation. I shared that I felt a little tired. I indicated to the doctor that after much thought, I had changed my mind about the left lung. I shared with him that I preferred to have a tissue sample obtained immediately and sent for biopsy especially given my family history as well as my history. He understood the underlying reasons for my concerns and agreed.

I have found that in this journey, there is a curveball thrown at you at almost every corner. The mistake I made was assuming that as I approached each corner, all would be behind me, and life would return to the normal that I wanted and expected. I found that I had to learn to rejoice in the moment because I could not see around that next corner.

Left Lung Cancer and Radiation Treatment

So here I was with a new track to be added to the roller-coaster ride. This ride was going to continue on for a while longer.

Dr. FV explained that intervention radiology would be the department responsible for the procedure used to obtain the tissue sample of my left lung. The EBUS procedure was not an option because the location of this nodule was at the top of my left lung. The process involved placing me in a twilight sleep and inserting a needle just below my shoulder to where the nodule was and obtain a sample. This would also be done during a real-time CT scan. Like the right lung, this process was very quick, and I was home within a few hours. Again, the necessary referral was obtained from my primary care provider, and the procedure was scheduled and held on December 20, 2018. Here we are at the holidays again.

Christmas was wonderful. I thoroughly enjoyed the decorations and dinner. On Thursday, December 27, 2018, we met with Dr. FV to get the results from the biopsy. The bad news was that the tissue tested positive for adenocarcinoma. The good news was that it was in the early stages. The staging was T1a N0 M0. This meant that the tumor was larger than 0.1 cm but not greater than 0.5 cm. Also, there was no lymph node involvement and no metastasis. This was also a primary cancer. So here I was with my third diagnosis of a cancer unrelated to the other cancers. The doctor explained that SABR treatment would also be his recommended course of treatment as was done with the right lung. I would need five treatments. I agreed, and plans were made. My treatment began about four weeks thereafter.

Right before we started treatments, I had another PET scan of my lungs and abdomen. The abdomen looked great, and the right lung tumor lit up to 3.8, so we were headed in the right direction from the treatment. It is not unusual for the effects of radiation to take some time to work. Hopefully, the left lung would respond as well.

After completion of my treatment, I had a follow-up visit with the oncologist. As with all oncology appointments, we discussed any side effects I may have experienced. We also discussed when I would need to have my scans.

The one burning question I had for the doctor was what treatment options would be available to me if the SABR treatment did not work. Was I out of nonsurgical options? He advised that depending on the changes in the tumor, SABR treatment might be acceptable and doable. A couple of other treatments could be radio frequency ablation (RFA) treatment or microwave ablation treatment. I came home and researched these two radiotherapy treatments just in case.

My oncologist stated there was no reason to consider other options as the last scans showed healing in the right direction. My experience taught me to ask the questions when you think of them. You never know when that information will become extremely important. I felt confident in his assessment, but given my history, I am a skeptic. The more professional explanation would be that I suffer from post-traumatic stress disorder. My guard never goes down completely. I also asked why the difference in how each lung tumor lit up on the PET scan since they were similarly staged. He explained that the right tumor was "angrier" than the left tumor. I can only assume that the left lung tumor was "sleepier."

My next scans were scheduled for April 25, 2019. Call me paranoid, but I was concerned that there were no recent scans of my brain. I also know that lung cancer will usually spread to the brain, and although there was no evidence of metastasis, my red flag was raising. So the insurance approval was obtained and the referral order issued. There would be an MRI of my brain and a CT scan of my lungs and abdomen. Both scans were completed, and I jumped for joy at the results. My brain was normal, and outside of a little scar tissue in my lung, the original mass was gone.

Listen to your instinct. It costs you nothing to ask that testing not be delayed. However, delaying the testing could change the outcome of your life. You have every right to ask. Insurance can even deny you. But there is always an appeal process, and I felt my health and family history would support their approving the brain scan.

Diving Grand Bahamas after radiation
of both lungs in June 2019.

Genetics Testing

We all have the kitchen drawer at home that has everything in it that you have been looking for and cannot find. It's the place we throw items that we forgot to put away: extra bolts, nuts, and screws that we don't know what to do with and pens and pencils. It is the drawer you go to when you can't find something in its proper place. Our body is similar to the drawer except it holds all the pieces and parts of our living body. In that body are many things, which include the genes that determine our biological fate and are influenced not only by external factors such as the environment but also by what we put into by our bodies either by the food we eat, the drugs we take, or the smoke we inhale. Genetic testing is also an avenue to discover what cancer we may be predisposed to developing. Although the general consensus is that genetics contributes only about 5 percent to 10 percent to the risk of developing cancer, I can only imagine that when added to my history of developing three primary cancers and the number of family members who have had cancer, how much that risk increases.

Shortly after commencing chemotherapy treatments, my chemo oncologist had reviewed my family history and was alarmed at the number of cancers in my immediate family, namely, a grandfather, one uncle, four aunts, and four cousins. The strong cancer history was on my mother's side of family. Amazingly, my mother, father, and sister never developed cancer. Many times, I felt that because of this, I was safe. Made perfect sense. How wrong that thinking proved to be. My doctor suggested that I move forward with genetic testing. She recommended a geneticist within my insurance network, and I waited for the approval from insurance, received a referral, and made the appointment.

We met the geneticist and found her to be very knowledge-able and accommodating. She gave my husband and me a wonderful explanation of this type of testing and what results we could expect to receive. The information is overwhelming, and genetic testing is a newer field that is constantly evolving. Again, asking questions is the key. Don't expect to become an expert in this field. You'll understand the basic information as it applies to your situation.

I'm only aware of one lab in California that does this type of test-ing. It takes roughly one month for the geneticist to receive a report. Patience is the key. For some reason, even though my insurance com-pany gave a preliminary approval, the process was held up, and the geneticist needed to provide additional information to the insurance company. It is a very costly test. Final approval was received, and my sample was shipped off to the lab in California. Because of the delay, it took an additional two months to finally complete this process.

In the early spring of 2018, the geneticist phoned to let me know we needed to meet to discuss the results. A week later, my hus-band and I met with her.

I was told that I did have a mutation in the NBN gene, which is linked to a risk in breast cancer. This gene mutation is different from the BRCA1 and BRCA2 genes that are more commonly related to an increased risk in breast cancer. As in the other mutations, this also contributes to a breakdown in the check and balance system within our cells. This mutation is found in eastern Europeans, and that is my heritage. Although the NBN gene mutation is noted for an increased risk in breast cancer, it can also be responsible for ovar-ian cancer and pancreatic cancer. Since my ampullary carcinoma is a subcategory under pancreatic cancer, I cannot help but wonder if this gene mutation was a determining factor in developing the ampullary carcinoma.

Since women with an NBN gene mutation have an increased risk of developing breast cancer, the recommendation was that my breast exams be held twice a year, alternating between a breast MRI and a general mammogram screening. I made this change to my preventative health maintenance. Thankfully to date, my breast exams have been normal. But I am always suspect and because of PTSD, I anticipate the radiologist will deliver bad news. I still live with the feeling that it will happen. I just don't know when.

Another important fact is that estrogen, which is produced by the ovaries, feeds cancer cells. Although I have the gene mutation for breast cancer, several years earlier, I had to have a total hysterectomy, which included the removal of my ovaries. I am hoping this is a blessing in disguise.

The second item from this test revealed that I did not have Lynch syndrome. As was explained to me, Lynch syndrome is a type of inherited cancer syndrome associated with different types of cancers but more commonly colon cancer. For example, you will see this when multiple relatives on the same side of the family develop colorectal cancer. You can also see this type of connection in endometrial cancer as well as some other cancers. People with Lynch syndrome are most likely to be diagnosed at a younger age and can also be at an increased risk of developing multiple types of cancers during their lifetime. I was glad that I did not have Lynch syndrome.

As we left the meeting, she said that she would keep in touch if any of the information provided to me had been improved upon. I feel this test is well worth taking and, at the suggestion of my geneticist, advised my immediate family that they should consider this as well. I leave that to them.

If you find that there is a gene mutation, you have the knowledge to share with your medical team so that an informed decision can be made as to what routine testing should be done and how often so that any change in your health can be discovered and treated early. Again, I cannot stress enough the importance of early intervention.

My Role as a Caregiver

Caregiving is such a demanding role, and it was not until I became responsible for the care and well-being of my sister that I began to understand the monumental responsibility I had. My mom and dad were from an era where you looked after your own family. My grandparents were from eastern Europe, and that was the mind-set as well, given the life in poverty that existed during their lifetime. Years ago, individuals born with disabilities were either cared for by the family or sent to live in government institutions that offered no quality of life. So it was ingrained in me from an early age that I was solely responsible for my sister's care. There is no doubt that my parents never entertained that I would suffer catastrophic illnesses or predecease my sister. So they never pursued an alternate living arrangement for her. Quite frankly, they could not afford it. I was always cautioned by my medical team to remove as much stress from my life as possible. Being a caregiver, as I would soon discover, is extremely stressful when you add my health issues, and thankfully, I was already in counseling.

In September 2010, my sister moved in with us. Over the course of the nine years my sister lived with us, I quickly learned that being a caregiver was more than providing meals and a roof. I also had to take into account that my sister needed mental stimulation, physical activities, and a social life. The two health clubs I was teaching at had several group exercise programs geared toward seniors. So I would take her with me on the days I taught. It worked well for the couple days a week I taught, but what about the other five days?

One thing that stands out in my mind is I had always promised myself I would not become my mother. Sandy was my sister, and I was not her mother. I needed to find that balance in my role as a caregiver but not as a mother. There is an old saying, "You are what you know." How true that is. I knew my sister felt lost, so I would take her everywhere with me, be it grocery shopping, having lunch with friends, seeing a movie, etc. In addition, when she first moved into our home, I gave up my closet so that she could have her own personal closet space. That was the beginning of the end. Like my mother, I found that I was losing my individuality. As much as I didn't want to become my mother, it was all I knew, so it became the path of least resistance. My mother never recognized it, but I did. I also never realized that my mother and my sister were two people in one person. When mom passed on December 25, 2008, my sister stepped into her shoes and mechanically continued to do the simple things to keep my dad comfortable. Once dad passed in March 2010, my sister lost her identity. The role she fulfilled on my mother's behalf was no longer needed. So I had to not only manage her reality, but I had to first create it.

In order to regain control of my individuality, in 2015, I moved my sister into the middle bedroom, which had a small closet. In addition, I purchased a small wardrobe for her to use. I took back possession of my larger closet. I continued to take her with me to the health clubs when I taught; however, I no longer took her with me to visit with friends. Our township provides transportation services for individuals who have no way of getting to the grocery store or to doctors' appointments. It took a couple of trips, but she eventually gained confidence and was able to make her own arrangements. She was becoming a little more independent. Slowly, I began to find myself. I suffered a great deal of guilt each time I made plans without her, but I knew it was the right decision. I also learned to balance my marriage with my caregiving responsibilities. There were certain times my husband and I would make plans that did not include her. Some occasions we did include her. It was never easy.

My husband and I also learned that disagreements and important discussions would take place over lunch, during a ride in the car, or sitting in the yard. It is amazing that in spite of disabilities, my sister did not miss a conversation. It did not matter if she was in the same room with us or not. Somehow, she heard our conversations. I certainly did not need her intertwined in my marital life of more than forty years. That is certainly a recipe for disaster.

Sandy had very poor balance. As the years passed, her balance worsened, and in mid-November 2016, while walking in the garage, she stumbled and fell breaking her left wrist. This happened approximately two weeks after having my gallbladder removed. Because of her disabilities, it was extremely difficult for her to function with a broken wrist. She was not a candidate for surgery as she suffered severe osteoporosis from the years of being on medications. So my healing from surgery became secondary, and she now became the top priority in my life. About a year and a half later, in May 2018, she was at the gym walking down the stairs, mis-stepped, and fell. We went to emergency care, and she needed stitches above her eye and at the top of her forehead. In June 2018, she developed an intestinal bug, and between the diarrhea and her diuretic medication, she dehydrated, and we almost lost her. We went by ambulance, and she was hospitalized for three days. Two months later in August 2018, she was getting out of the bathtub, and her hand slipped on the ledge. She broke her right wrist. Another visit to emergency care and another six weeks of her not being able to function. Two of the incidences in 2018 occurred during my chemotherapy treatments. With my lowered blood counts from chemo, my immune system was compromised so the last place I needed to be was in a hospital exposed to viruses and bacterial infections. My stress was off the charts. I became painfully aware of the fact that she needed to be relocated to a senior community that would provide a safer environment, meet all her needs, and provide her an opportunity to thrive. And let's not forget my guilt at having to make this decision.

Before each occurrence, I would suggest to Sandy that she needed to take precautions to keep herself safe in her daily activities. Although we did not have a walk-in tub, we did have a shower bench for her to use. She was adamant about not using it. I used to believe that she did not want to take my advice because I was her younger sister. But as I look back, I really believe it was more of a desire to make her own decisions, be them bad or good, and to reach for some independence. I wish I would have started the relocation process after the first broken wrist, but again, there was that guilt issue. Hindsight is twenty-twenty.

When I had my first cancer diagnosis, I realized that the little bit of estate planning my husband and I did when it came to my sister was minimal. Unfortunately, there was not enough time before my Whipple surgery to get my affairs in order as they related to her continued care. I am sure that this unfinished business is one of the items that inspired me to get through the surgery and healing process. Although I had visited some senior communities prior to surgery, I still had not found the one that I was totally comfortable with. Shortly after returning to work, my manager and I chatted. She shared information about a senior community that her dad had been placed in and how pleased the family was with the facility. As with my sister, her father had limited financial means. Options are not abundant when you are not a person of means. I made an appointment and took my sister to tour the community. I wanted her involved in the process so that she could feel that her opinion was important. My criterion was that if I would live in the community, then it would be a good fit for Sandy.

It was an extremely clean facility. Meals and snacks were provided. Each apartment had a kitchenette that was shared by two people with each person having their own private bedroom and bath. Activities were offered each day, and religious services were held weekly. Apartments were cleaned each week, and laundry facilities were available or you could have laundry done once a week by staff. There was a beauty shop on site, and the prices were more than reasonable. A podiatrist visits monthly and a medical doctor visits weekly to assist individuals with their medical needs. The community provides day trips from time to time for those individuals who are mobile. Monthly trips to the local stores are also provided. Emergency cords were provided in each bedroom along with basic satellite television. This was everything I had hoped for. My sister was placed on the waiting list. She was number six. It took almost nine months for her to take the number one spot and move in. In May 2019, she moved in.

The most important thing for me was that my sister would have all her needs met—housing, food, socialization, activities, and personal needs. It is amazing how different people in your life are there for a reason. Thank you to my manager for sharing this information.

Although my sister has disabilities, she could function in a controlled environment such as this offered. This living arrangement would give her an opportunity to thrive, and I volunteered to offer a senior moves exercise class once a week for six weeks to help her make friends. I wanted to do everything possible to help her in this transition. Up until this time, my mother had been her only friend. I never had to teach the class but would have pursued doing so if she had not adjusted well.

As pleased as I was with the new community, it was still difficult for me. Since I was already in counseling, I addressed my issues as a caregiver during my sessions. I learned that I needed to let my sister make some minor mistakes so that she could learn. I began shifting the responsibility of simple decision-making to her so that she could develop the ability to somewhat look after herself. It is a fine line to know when I need to interfere and when I need to let her work her way through things, but counseling helped us both a great deal.

To prepare Sandy for her new life, each day I would take an example and turn the event into a life lesson. Whether it was a news story or a television program, I would apply the situation to her and teach her what would be a safe decision and what would not be. I do not believe that my parents would be disappointed. In one of our counseling sessions, I learned that Sandy had some feelings of abandonment from when I got married, which I never knew about. I assured her, as did the therapist, that the changes to her life were for the better and not because I was abandoning her. I explained to her that if any of my scans were not good, I wanted peace of mind knowing that she would be living her life well. I believe she eventually understood.

It is such a blessing to find that the government realized people need to thrive in these communities. I know my mother and father never envisioned that this could be possible. I am at peace with my decision, and I know in my heart that my parents are happy. I am so glad that they did not live long enough to see the battles with cancer I have had to endure. It would have destroyed them. Everything happens for a reason, and I have faith. Every day I do miss having my sister with us. Let me make one thing clear—I don't miss the stress and neither does she.

Through this process, I learned to be more patient with individuals who have disabilities. I learned to recognize that persons with disabilities have their strong points and weak points. These individuals are also very proud. Promote their strong points, and help them to overcome their weaknesses not by criticism but by positive reinforcement. Their learning capacity varies, and coping skills might not be strong. Take that into consideration, and teach them through baby steps. If it is not overwhelming, you will find that they enjoy learning things.

Spiritual Journey

Religion is a very sensitive topic. It is said that the two subjects you should avoid talking about in a group setting are religion and politics. When it comes to religion, there will always be those nay-sayers. I have always believed that it is healthy to question one's religious beliefs as that is what opens the pathway of communication with God. What I have discovered is that God is very real as are his religious teachings. From a common sense point of view, God has withstood the test of time, and Christianity is thriving throughout the world. I need no other proof.

What is equally important is that our spiritual healing runs parallel with our physical healing. As a result, your pastor, minister, etc. should be an integral part of your medical team. You should have faith in your spiritual guide and feel confident that he can lead you on the right path with God.

Long before my diagnoses, I had already longed for a reconnection with my faith. I never stopped loving God, but attending church was not something I had done regularly for a long time. After retiring in May 2013, I made it a point to address my spiritual unrest and began attending mass regularly. It brought a great deal of peace to my soul, and it was a good start in my spiritual journey. At about that same time, my parish was looking for religious education instructors.

I chatted with the manager of the program and shared my concern for not having had a formal Bible education. She assured me that the lesson plans were designed so it would not be difficult to teach the class. Maybe this was my calling. I taught for three years but found myself feeling incompetent as an instructor. There is no formal type of training. I found some of the fifth graders I taught to be smarter than me in the Bible events, and so I discontinued teaching after three years. It was just as well as I was becoming quite ill at the time. Maybe it was divine intervention.

Still somewhat lost in my spiritual journey, I looked to find solace from the scripture and gospel readings during mass. It helped but wasn't the cure for my unrest. I would visit one of the local churches during the day and chat with God. That helped me a great deal. Now, as I look back, divine intervention was probably the reason for my cancers. I know that sounds absurd, but I believe everything that happens to us has a much higher purpose. In Hebrews 11:1, it is written: "Now faith is being sure of what we hope for and certain of what we do not see." I needed to believe in God and in my faith, and I knew this was a higher calling to get my life in order. You do not see, but you just know. It also taught me that I needed to learn from the scriptures and expand my communication with God.

When diagnosed for the very first time in September 2017, I was so angry at God. Even though this diagnosis felt like my road to hell, it was also my road to deepening and strengthening my faith in God. I would stop in at church and have in-depth conversations with God. I even argued with Him. One thing I learned from teaching religious education is that a conversation with God doesn't have to be by formal prayer. I let Him know in no uncertain terms that I felt my illness was unfair; I did not deserve this. There are murderers sitting in jail, and yet I am delivered what might be a death sentence. After all, there was still so much unfinished business I needed to address. Now was not a good time for me to die. It was simply out of the question.

I remember going to confession and sharing with the priest that I questioned God as to "why me." I felt so abandoned. But I also shared that I loved him. And Father very simply stated: "Did Jesus ask, 'Why me?'" That certainly gave me pause for thought. In Psalms 22:2, Jesus cries, "My God, my God, why have you abandoned me? Why so far from my call for help, from my cries of anguish?" Like me, Jesus questioned why God abandoned him. In Psalms 22:4, Jesus says, "Yet you are enthroned as the Holy One; you are the glory of Israel." Even in His most desperate hour, Jesus recognized that only God has power over life. And so, I needed to direct my conversations and prayers directly with God. He certainly has the power of life over me, and I needed to believe that he would do what was best for me.

The scriptures are how we learn and connect with God. But I read the scriptures and did not understand them. I wasn't born during the time they were written, and that is part of the key to understanding them. My parish was beginning a Bible study program, a condensed version, for anyone wishing to become closer with God through His scriptures. I signed up. It was a very intense course. I have completed four so far and am learning to understand the messages behind scriptures. I find that my studies give me a greater sense of God and my purpose here on earth.

I needed to accept the fact that I was in God's hands. He is the giver and taker of life. I changed my conversations with Him and pleaded with Him to spare my life. I felt that my heart was pure and hoped he would see that as well. He must have as I am still here. Each day is special, and I don't take it for granted. Many of the reasons I gave when pleading my life to God, I am now working on. I am sure that as time passes, other important goals will be made known to me. I have certainly found more peace with where I am now in my spirituality, and I am enjoying a much richer life. I am not the same person I was before my illnesses, and I do not want to be that person. In the beginning, I wondered what would be said at my eulogy if things had played out differently. Hopefully, it would not be about the color of my appliances or the antique piano. I would hope that it would be that by example and kindness, I encouraged someone else to fight through their illness, to be strong, and to have faith in God. Life is precious, and I never realized how shallow we can become as human beings. There is nothing wrong with wanting nicer and better things as long as we stay true to God. Not an easy task but one we all face when challenged with possibly meeting Him sooner than we hoped. "Rejoice always" can be found in 1 Thessalonians 5:16. Two very simple words but really a difficult task. How could I rejoice in my illness?

As with the conventional therapy with which we are familiar, spiritual therapy is also available, at least in the Catholic faith. I had some very basic, but important, questions about our life with God while on this earth. It was an ad in our church bulletin with a description about pursuing spiritual counseling. I had my answer. Call it divine intervention again, but I knew I needed to obtain spiritual counseling. It was my decision to pursue a counseling session at a church other than my parish. It was not a reflection on my parish just a reflection on what I was comfortable with. My counseling session lasted almost one and a half hours. I left invigorated and with a better understanding of my relationship with God.

As my Bible studies continue and as I try to follow my path as a good Christian, I am sure my faith will deepen as well.

We all have to believe in something of a higher power, or there would be no purpose to live your life as a Christian. It is almost impossible to not reach for God in a catastrophic crisis. It is during these times that I have learned we are all at the mercy of God or the higher power chosen by other faiths. I also believe that miracles are small but there. Just open your eyes and really see around you. Each day I wake up is a miracle. The fact that I have been successful in managing my cancer diagnoses is a miracle. Driving my car safely each day is a miracle. Laughing and arguing with my family is a miracle. My life is a miracle, and I have found that some new doors have opened in the way of support work as a cancer volunteer. As did God's apostles that are so evident in the Acts of the Apostle, so I too have a mission that is becoming clearer as each day passes. At almost sixty-six years of age, I have a lot of yesterdays but few tomorrows. I live each day as if it were my last. I waste a lot less time worrying about what tomorrow will bring because it is not in my hands to control. I know that each day I am blessed. I will never lose sight of that again. So yes, I have learned to rejoice always because of the person that I have now become.

What's important to note that regardless of the faith you practice, recognize that you are in God's hands, and the most important gift that your family and friends can give you is a gift of prayer. God hears and listens. He listens to them and to you. Prayers work. I am living proof of that. Believe. Each day you survive is a win because none of us really have tomorrow guaranteed to us. We cannot understand that unless we put aside our arrogance.

If my life were condensed and placed on a reel of film, what I know in my heart is that there are several blank frames at the end of the reel. They have yet to be filled with my life's moments. I know based on my faith that I still have work that needs to be completed. When that is done and the film is ready for viewing, my life will be complete, and I will be ready for my new chapter with God. I cannot see this nor can I prove this, but with faith, I believe. My life still needs an ending to my life script.

It is amazing that I began to really feel my body begin the healing process when I returned to teaching aqua aerobics during chemotherapy. I cannot help but recognize the parallel between healing from teaching water aerobics and the water used when we are baptized into a life with God because it is through the waters of baptism that we are healed from the sins of our ancestors.

Your Private Space

We have all experienced that time in our life when we are conducting a conversation or completing a business transaction and the person behind us in line fails to respect the circle of private space around us. There have also been many instances where I have witnessed individuals correct someone for not being respectful of their private space. The circle around each of us is an area of space that lets us decide who or what can safely enter our life. It also determines who or what should not enter our life.

As I embarked on my cancer journey and as the twists and turns became more difficult, I found that I needed to take an inventory of who and what I had allowed into my life. My healing depended on this. It is not an easy task because some of those people who should not be in our life may very well be family members. Unfortunately, not all family members get along.

The individuals whom you allow into your life and into your private space are paramount to the success of your healing journey. When it comes to friends, most of us have already determined who is truly a friend. But there are individuals you need to disassociate from because they leave you feeling exhausted. When you do remove them from your life, do it diplomatically and with kindness. They more than likely have their own struggles and do not even realize the negative impact they have on the people around them. There will always be individuals who come in and out of your life. Sometimes our paths change as do the paths of these individuals. That is normal. However, when it comes to family, things become more problematic.

Ideally all family members get along, and everything is wonderful. But that is not reality. And because of family dynamics, we usually can't just send them away. The key here is to avoid family gatherings that might erupt into a combative event. Do not take phone calls from them or, if you have to, keep the conversations short. Distance yourself at family events that cannot be avoided and surround yourself with the family members who are supportive.

Then there are those situations where even distancing yourself from an individual family member is not enough. You do need to permanently remove them from your life. If the family member happens to be related to your spouse or significant other, it is their responsibility as your caregiver and partner to intervene and create the boundaries with their family members so that you can heal. It will never be pleasant, but sometimes it is necessary. Your recovery and healing depend on it. You may not get a second chance. Don't ignore the signs. In our case, my husband's family's dysfunction was fueled by hate and control. We would have preferred to stay and grow as part of the family unit, but early on, we knew it was not meant to be. There were more recent incidences that involved some extended family, and sadly, we were faced with the same decision. These individuals have bred this same hate and dysfunction within their own families. It is these few individuals that will try to derail your efforts to seek counseling and possibly other unconventional methods that you may choose as part of your healing process. Although it is always preferred to preserve the family unit, life isn't perfect, and sometimes we have to make those difficult choices. It is okay to do that. You celebrate family when the family unit is developed from positive interactions and shared experiences. Without that, family is nothing more than genetics. That doesn't mean that there won't be some minor disagreements, but true family is forgiving, nonjudgmental, and gives unconditional love. They don't use those minor disagreements to fuel hate. Do what you have to do to save yourself. Look at it simply as setting your boundaries.

Exercise or Not?

We have all been exposed to Internet, television, and newspaper ads depicting perfectly fit individuals promoting gym memberships and new types of exercise equipment. There seem to be as many fads in the fitness industry as there are in the clothing industry. It is so abundant that these ads have little impact on individuals who were not born with the perfect weight, height, bone structure, health, and figure. I believe these ads can sometimes be counterproductive. People are like those items that we find in the kitchen drawer that contains a little bit of everything. They come in different shapes and sizes and with different health issues and risks.

Based on my position in the fitness industry, I believe that the new normal is the aging population. Most of us will enjoy longevity. Unfortunately, with longevity comes the fact that we will develop catastrophic illnesses. It cannot be avoided. I am so grateful to have had the support of two fitness centers that strive to bring in professionals who have the specialty training to bring to the public. Although in their infancy stages, both fitness centers, Orland Park Health & Fitness Center, which is under the management of Power Wellness, and Tinley Fitness, are the new paradigm of how fitness facilities should approach health and well-being. Both fitness facilities strive to provide the special populations with tailored programming. However, there still needs to be staff who are certified to work with those populations who have been diagnosed and are combatting a catastrophic illness such as cancer. The director of Tinley Fitness does an incredible job of welcoming new specialty programs proposed by her staff that will not only benefit the fitness center but, more importantly, will benefit the members and the community. The future of fitness is changing and rightfully so. I am very fortunate to have survived my illnesses so that I can bring positivity and guidance to the members and my clients.

To support my belief that the exercise industry needs to become more specialized, the United States Census Bureau released a press release on March 13, 2018, addressing the accelerated growth in the senior population. The release states that

> [B]y 2030, all baby boomers will be older than age 65. This will expand the size of the older population so that 1 in every 5 residents will be retirement age… "By 2034…there will be 77.0 million…people 65 years and older."[3]

In a report issued by the United States Bureau of Labor Statistics,

> By 2024, BLS projects that the labor force will grow to about 164 million people. That number includes about 41 million people who will be ages 55 and older—of whom about 13 million are expected to be ages 65 and older.

The report further states that "although they make up a smaller number of workers overall, the 65- to 74-year-old age groups are projected to have faster rates of labor force growth annually than any

---

[3] "Older People Projected to Outnumber Children for First Time in U.S. History," US Census Bureau, March 13, 2018, rev. Sept. 6, 2018 and Oct. 8, 2019, accessed January 17, 2020.

other age groups."[4] The fitness industry needs to redesign their programs, and staff their facilities with specialized individuals to meet the needs of the aging population.

Another member of your healing team should be a personal trainer to help you in your healing journey. This individual will share equal importance with your spiritual guide, therapist, and medical doctors. When interviewing a fitness professional to add to your team, you will always want to ask the usual questions such as, how long they have been in the fitness industry, what specialized training they have undergone, etc. But the most important response you want to hear from a fitness professional is that they will review the information you have provided and devise a plan to address the issues you have that relate to your illness and any treatments you have had or are currently undergoing. If they are able to provide a workout from their memory, then they are not the right fit for you. I say this because of my certification through the Cancer Exercise Training Institute. The institute continuously posts new information in the cancer field that may be beneficial to a client. There are always new discoveries in the field, and a little research will go a long way to creating a plan that will benefit my client. A good fitness professional will do their research in order to provide you with the best possible exercise program. Hold them to the same high standard that you hold your doctors, therapist, and spiritual advisor. Always remember that your fitness specialist is a secondary caregiver.

As a personal trainer and group fitness instructor who specializes in Parkinson's disease, multiple sclerosis, and cancer fitness, I approach health from a realistic point of view. I stated earlier that the fitness industry is slowly evolving, and rightfully so, into specialized fields. A good instructor has no ego, knows it is a continual learning process, strives to give their best at each class or personal training session, and works as part of a team sharing ideas with their coworkers as part of their learning process. I also believe that a good

---

4 "Older workers: Labor force trends and career options," Miltra Toossi and Elka Torpey, US Bureau of Labor Statistics, May 2017, accessed January 17, 2020.

instructor knows their weaknesses, embraces them, and stays within their expertise.

Because of my thought process about the fitness industry, I take a common sense approach to fitness. In group classes, I look at the demographics. I am the professional. My job is to look professional, dress professional, and create a safe exercise program for the class and my clients. After all, they trust that what I am asking them to do is safe. It is not about me; it is about them. Many of the individuals who regularly attend my classes have overcome some severe illnesses. There is no doubt that their commitment to staying fit has played a key role. The class setting is perfect for those who seek peer support and camaraderie and who have returned to a fully functional life. For a monthly membership fee at a gym, most classes offered will be included. Many gyms accept Silver Sneakers, which is paid for by your insurance if your insurance has a contract with them. However, when you are first recovering from a cancer diagnoses or surgery and treatment, one-on-one with a personal trainer would be the first logical step after any physical therapy needed and approval from your doctors.

Once your fitness center has paired you with a fitness professional, that individual should sit down with you, go over your restrictions, if any, and list your medications and the type of cancer involved, any surgery, types of treatment, and if lymphedema is or was present. That professional will take your information, and when you meet for your first session, your exercise plan will be presented to you so that you can ask questions and understand the benefits of the program designed for you. As with all of your professional team members, if this individual does not resonate for you, then ask for a different individual. After all, this is your journey, and you need to have faith and confidence in each member of your team.

It is important to note that adults who endured childhood cancer can still suffer the effects from surgery and treatment many years down the road. So a fitness professional needs to be mindful of that fact and watch for the signs and symptoms. Some individuals who were very active and extremely fit before their illness may want to pick up where they left off. That is just not possible nor is it wise. As a cancer survivor, it is always best to start slow and easy and build up. Impatience will not be your friend but can be your enemy.

I want to dispel the rumors that only skinny people are healthy and safe from disease. This is just not true. Being fit means that your body has the ability to function efficiently and effectively in work and play. It also means that you bring strength to fighting this disease and that you have improved your ability to recover from this catastrophic illness.

If you are inactive, you will not have the cardiorespiratory fitness needed to withstand surgery and recovery. Nor will you have the stamina to persevere in your healing journey. One of the issues deals with excessive fat tissue when looking at body mass and the effect that tissue has on your joints, bones, and major organs. You can have excessive fat tissue and not necessarily be grossly obese. Let's add the cancer diagnosis. The stamina to make it through surgery and each chemo and radiation treatment really depends on how fit you are. If a cancer patient needs surgery to remove infected tissue or organs and lymph nodes, the risk of lymphedema is elevated because fat tissue creates excess fluid, and those lymph nodes are no longer available to expel the fluid in that area. Less fat tissue, less risk of lymphedema. This is not to be confused with edema. Edema is generally caused by excess fluid in the tissue that has not yet returned to the circulatory system; whereas, lymphedema is protein-rich lymph that is trapped within the tissue, and the lymph nodes needed to expel that fluid are no longer there because they have been removed or are unable to correct this imbalance because they are injured during surgery. As a cancer exercise professional, it is my job to create an exercise program that will provide movement that will not exacerbate the condition and work toward improving the condition. Left untreated, the tissue can become fibrotic and can also provide a medium for bacterial and fungal infections. There are many more serious complications that can occur. As if you don't have enough to overcome.

So yes, exercise is very important. Looking at my own journey, had I not been as active, I truly believe the outcome would have been different. It saved my life and accelerated the healing process for me, especially when I went back to teaching while on chemotherapy.

Exercise doesn't have to be a regimented schedule in a gym. You can exercise by joining a walking group, bike-riding group, bird-watching group, etc. The various opportunities are abundant. Exercise should not be a choice but should be a part of your treatment, just as chemotherapy and radiation and counseling are. Even if you have never exercised, you have nowhere to go but up.

Think about this for one moment. The most important reason to exercise and stay fit is to put your body in the best position to let you know that something is seriously wrong. When an individual is inactive and unfit, they develop so many minor health issues, what's one more? Most times, catastrophic illnesses present their symptoms very subtly. The symptoms blend with all the other symptoms. When the body is working optimally, it will let you know that something is extremely wrong because I truly believe our bodies like being fit.

Don't short-change yourself. Life is a beautiful gift from God. Cherish it by keeping fit. Find that professional to work with you and assist you in recovering from your illness. There are thirty-minute personal training sessions that is the perfect length of time to begin your exercise program until you can build up your stamina. Training sessions in the pool can be better tolerated and easier on your body. The water has wonderful healing properties. Plus, if your balance has been affected, you will not get hurt should you fall during your exercise session. The water is very forgiving. Speak with your medical team about entering an exercise program. Let them list your limitations for the exercise professional. You may feel that you cannot afford a personal trainer even for a limited time. But the reality is you can't afford not to hire a fitness professional. It can be a great birthday or holiday gift idea. Don't put this on hold for tomorrow. Remember, the only thing certain is today.

Another minor point that needs to be addressed has to do with recovery. As things currently stand, insurance companies will approve physical therapy for individuals that will bring you to a point where you can accomplish your activities of daily living (ADL). However, given the statistics by our own government that I cited to earlier in this chapter, I think that individuals need to receive physical therapy and sessions with a personal trainer so that they can enjoy a fully functional life (FFL). A fully functional life will be unique to each individual. Simply stated, ADL refers to the very basic functions of living. You can feed yourself, clean yourself after using the bathroom, dress yourself, and have some mobility. I define a fully functional life as being able to enjoy leisure activities and having the ability to enter or reenter the workforce. As things stand right now, these last two items are much more problematic. Given the statistics, this has to change. Instead of being able to perform the simplest activities of daily living, we should be able to enjoy a fully functional life limited only by the residue of a catastrophic illness or disease. Otherwise, what would be the point of longevity? More importantly, as a society, we are responsible for taking care of and protecting our most vulnerable populations.

Ideally and if legally possible, the future of fitness should be represented by a consortium between the local community fitness centers and the medical community to create a facility for people to work with the professional fitness industry. In this way, we can serve our local communities and assist individuals in their continuation of care after surgery, or treatment, or physical therapy has ended. This would create a dedicated environment designed to assist people in continuing their journey. It would show that the local fitness and medical communities are vested in the communities they serve.

It is important to note that unless the fitness industry raises its bar, it will never hold a standing in the health community as being a necessary part of an individual's journey to well-being. To accomplish this, there needs to be transparency, a standardization of education requirements, and accountability. This can only be accomplished by creating, at the very least, a state registration board that would promulgate the rules and oversee the legitimacy of the industry. Until then, fitness centers are nothing more than fancy gyms.

Let's not forget that our senior citizen population will generally have the disposable income to support our economy. They also return to the work force as part-time workers, which helps the smaller businesses out as they do not have to pay benefits. Most important, they keep our history and cultures alive.

Reflections

As I look back at my journey, there is so much I have learned. Here are those important reflections that I hope will aid you in your journey.

Reflection 1: I have such a great admiration for family care-givers who approach their responsibility with love. It's easy to be a caregiver from afar, write the checks, and visit occasionally. But it takes a special individual to accept someone in your home and make them a part of your daily life. I was far from the ideal example of what a caregiver should be. I had no direction and never understood my sister's disabilities until after I met with her doctor and discussed her health issues at length. I was ill-prepared to fulfill my role. But I have also learned to forgive myself for my inadequacies for I feel that I did the best I could under the circumstances. If nothing else, I hope my experience sheds some light on how to maneuver through the ups and downs of caregiving. Forgive yourself, and be at peace with the best you can do.

Reflection 2: Be patient with your caregivers. Like you, your family is doing the best they can do. They are not in your shoes, but you are not in their shoes. It is easy to get angry with them, but they can only do what you want if you share it with them. Don't expect them to be mind readers. They have your best interest at heart, and this is a learning curve for them just as dealing with your cancer has been a learning curve for you. Recognize that. If they ask you a question, answer it sincerely. Don't expect them to read between the lines.

Reflection 3: I nurtured my faith in God. In spite of my anger, I do believe that my cancer journey was to prepare me for a greater role. I never knew what faith in God was until I had to face the graveness of my situation, especially given the low success rate of Whipple surgery. I pleaded in my prayers to God to spare my life as I had so much important unfinished business especially when it came to my sister. In my spiritual counseling, I learned that although you cannot negotiate with God, he does listen if your request is sincere, your heart is pure, and it is for the greater good of all. I will always believe that. Without faith, you have no compass to fight for your life. I also have come to believe that nothing is etched in stone. God has the power over life and can change whatever He wants. Sometimes what He gives us is not the outcome we want or expect, and if it isn't, we have to rely on our faith that this is what is best for us. But there are times when you feel God is giving you that additional time. Cherish it. It truly is a gift from God. When in doubt, quiet your mind and listen with your heart. God is there.

Reflection 4: Because of my cancer battles, I chose to volunteer as a mentor for a cancer support group, Imerman's Angels. Healing comes about in many different ways. For me, the volunteer work plays a role in my healing. There are many groups that provide great support for cancer patients. After researching, this was the support group that resonated for me. In this way, as a disciple of God, I can do His healing work. Another avenue of healing was looking for a group that was specific to the pancreatic cancer family and Whipple surgery patients. After researching the Internet, I found a Facebook group called Whipple Warriors. There were rules specific to being a member of this group such as no sales, no promotion of medical services, and no fundraising. This group is worldwide and has several thousand members that consist of patients and caregivers and continues to be a wonderful source of information relating to medications, symptoms, recurrences, etc. Experience is the best teacher, and who better than those who have come before you.

Reflection 5: Be kind to yourself. I held a lot of anger and blamed myself for the two lung cancers. After all, I was a smoker for forty years, and even though I had not smoked in several years, the damage was there. I was a product of the 1950s and 1960s. Everybody smoked, and by the time the adverse effects were discovered, I was already hooked. During those years, there wasn't too much attention paid to the warnings. After all, it was the government forcing the tobacco companies to place the warnings on the packages. As youngsters, we called it Big Brother control. There were still many television commercials influencing smokers. But I own my decision. I chose not to heed the warnings. I do hold myself accountable, but I have also learned to move past my guilt.

Reflection 6: Know and understand your health insurance. It will save a lot of stress and headaches as you travel this path. The most important item is to always receive a copy of your referrals. All referrals expire. Understand that referrals are good for either a certain number of visits or a certain date, whichever occurs first. There is nothing more aggravating than to arrive for your medical appointment and find that your referral expired. Now you are frantically trying to reach your primary care provider for the referral. Also look at the life insurance policy you have and whether or not it will serve the purpose when you are gone. Once you have been diagnosed with a catastrophic illness, life insurance companies can and will refuse you coverage should you wish to buy a new policy or merely increase the amount of the one you have. I know because I was denied an increase in my existing policy.

Reflection 7: Always receive a copy of your lab orders and test results from your doctor or the testing facility. You are entitled to it. Every blood test, MRI, CT scan, PET scan, outpatient procedure I had, I carried the medical orders and blood test results with me. It saves a lot of time and patience. I have had instances where medical facilities were unable to access blood test results from the lab owned by the same provider. The electronics age does not come without deficiencies. Be prepared.

Reflection 8: As you navigate through this journey, recognize when you need professional guidance and counseling. It is not a crime to suffer from depression and PTSD, but it is a crime not to seek help. You do not suffer alone because when you suffer, your loved ones suffer with you. It is not a popularity contest. Don't let the view that those around you have on depression influence your decision to seek professional help. Understand that PTSD and depression never go away, but how you manage it will make a difference in your recovery and the rest of your life. Do not let it define your life. I only suffer for a few fleeting moments now and then. I can live with that.

Reflection 9: Based on my upbringing, I was taught to never accept help because if I did accept help, then I was indebted to that person. I am not sure where that thought process came from, but I can tell you without a doubt, it is wrong. Do not be afraid to accept help from family and friends. Welcome their offer of help. If their offer was not genuine, they would not have made it. I found a new depth to my friendships and family and found their support and prayers to be a godsend. I hope I can be there some day for them should the need arise.

Reflection 10: Don't discard the efforts of your friends and family. All the days in the hospital post-surgery and even during my recovery at home, I let the depression rule and would not speak to anyone or let anyone visit. When people would call my husband, I had 1,001 excuses why I did not want visitors and conversation. Yet all the while, I was silently screaming, "Please come and visit with me!" How could they know? Even I did not understand why I was desperately thinking one way yet saying something so contrary. Surround yourself with your friends and family. They are your support.

Reflection 11: Be open with your medical team. Do not hold back when sharing your health issues. After all, they too are not mind readers. They cannot help you if they do not know. I did have cause to look for a new pulmonologist. My goal was to return to diving. I do not believe the pulmonologist I had researched dive medicine and may have prematurely approved me to scuba dive. I took my dive trip, and all turned out well. But there is some indication that I should not have been released. I will never know that answer, but thankfully, I did several dives without incidence. It was only later that I learned that just because the dives went well is not an indication that I should have been cleared to dive. Injury from the radiation could cause my lungs to fail at any time and not necessarily during the first few dives.

I also learned that each lung works independently so, for example, your left lung might function at 60 percent and your right at 40 percent. What does that mean for my diving? Since my left lung seems to be in fairly good working order, will it support my body if the right lung collapses while diving? Would a test showing each lung's functioning capacity help to make that determination? If placed at a dive depth in a recompression chamber with a CT scan, will the scan show how effectively I can withstand the pressure and avoid lung trauma? Will it show how well the lungs are holding up? These are questions I will always have. I have since found a new pulmonologist that seems to understand what I want. I am also consulting with a second pulmonologist who is well versed in dive medicine. A second opinion is always good. The jury is still out as to whether I can continue scuba diving, but we are hopeful and taking those necessary treatment steps that may allow me to realize my goal.

Reflection 12: When meeting with a doctor for the first time, use the consultation to interview the doctor and decide if this individual is a good fit. A good doctor treats his patients competently. A great doctor knows your goals, understands your concerns, and undertakes the responsibility to familiarize themselves with the particular treatments and testing that allow you to meet your expectations. If a doctor is not the right fit on your medical team, then find a new one, and do not feel one bit embarrassed by your decision. Your life is in their hands.

Reflection 13: Forgive yourself for feeling inferior because of this catastrophic illness. Cancer does not select victims based on age, race, sex, or religion. We produce cancer cells every day. Our cells have a check and balance system. Cancer cells are produced in certain cells, and when that production gets out of hand, there is a built-in system to have the cells die, keeping the cancer cells from multiplying out of control. When the DNA of our cells are altered for whatever reason, the cancer cells produce at a faster rate than can be controlled, and the self-destruct mechanism no longer works. So, an inequity develops in our check and balance system. It is not your fault. Since we cannot turn back the hands of time and change our lifestyle, we will never know what truly caused the change in our cells. Embrace it and use it as a tool to strengthen yourself. If you give up, the disease wins. The disease may win no matter what, but staying strong will give you quality of life. Never go down without a fight, and *never give up*. Understand that there are new treatments coming out every day. What looks hopeless today can become curable next week.

Reflection 14: With my first diagnosis of ampullary carcinoma, I was frustrated with the lack of information and treatment protocol available. I was also shocked at the cost of my chemotherapy. Thankfully, I had insurance. I don't blame the pharmaceutical companies for the lack of treatment protocols. It takes years for a pharmaceutical company to secure approval for a medication. These are considered the research and development years (R&D). The number of employees and expense incurred during these years must be staggering. You have scientists and doctors, as well as ancillary staff, that need to be paid for their work in this process before obtaining approval. There is no guarantee the medication will be approved for use. For rare cancers, there isn't enough of a customer base to recoup their initial research costs if approval is obtained. That does place a "dollars and cents" tag on lives, but that is the reality we live in. No matter what the business, a company needs to determine what their return on the investment will be. It keeps people employed.

We live in a litigious society. I have a great deal of respect for the legal community as a whole. But there are those who will take up any cause. The money is in class action lawsuits. There are many legitimate and important claims against companies for failing to meet safety and health standards. But I also believe that there is a good part of the public who feel that suing a company is their "get rich quick" ticket. So companies need to plan against potential class action lawsuits and build that into the price of medication. I don't pass judgment on the pharmaceutical industry.

Because of these preliminary catastrophic expenses, many patients will find that they cannot afford some medications. Some of the drug companies have avenues by which you can apply to obtain the medication at a reduced cost. Always check with the pharmaceutical company by accessing their website, or via phone, to see if there is an application process to apply for assistance with the medication, and if so, what you need to provide in the way of information. You will find they are more than willing to lend whatever assistance they can.

Reflection 15: Don't suffer from arrogance. Throughout my life, like everyone, I used what I call throw-away phrases. "Anyone can get cancer, but when it's my time to go, there is nothing I can do about it." "We all have to go some time." There are many. I no longer use those phrases. It's easy to blurt them out in a conversation, because when we are healthy, we do suffer from arrogance. We have no reality when it comes to the possibility of a catastrophic illness, and we believe that today is forever.

Reflection 16: I also recognize more than ever the importance of keeping fit. I am not implying that you have to be a fitness guru. Quite to the contrary, for most people, that is not realistic. Life has its own terms. However, develop good eating habits, keep moving, stay active, and find that positive mental attitude. If you do, your body will align itself and will become accustomed to feeling great. When an imbalance does occur, your body will let you know. It will provide you with those early signs and symptoms. Remember, the key to success is early intervention. And the key to early intervention is recognizing the signs your body is giving you because it likes being fit.

Reflection 17: Live in the now. I never quite understood that concept. The first time I learned to understand it was two and a half months into chemotherapy when I went back to teaching aqua aerobics. As I have stated, water is my strength just as water is used when we are baptized into a life with God. There is nothing wrong with planning for tomorrow. It's great to feel as though you can make those plans and work toward the future. However, remember that what you have is today. Live in the moment. Enjoy the day to its fullest because every day is a gift. Enjoy each day to its fullest, and take it one day at a time. We cannot control what tomorrow might bring, so why waste precious time on what we have no control over? Mahatma

Gandhi said it so wisely, "Live as if you were to die tomorrow. Learn as if you were to live forever."

To put it into perspective, if you were told that you had seven days to live, how would you play it forward for those seven days? If you were told you had seven days to relive your whole life, what would you do differently? Simply put, if the spouse, sibling, parent, or child sitting across from you at dinner were no longer here, what would be the last memory you would hope to have about them? Would it be texting on your cell phone or talking about their day and how things went? The answers you give to these questions should guide how you live your life on a daily basis. Since we cannot go back in time, we should play it forward wisely.

Reflection 18: I look at my experiences, bad and good, differently. Experiences shape who we are and also serve to strengthen us. I learned that cancer is strong, but I am stronger. If I am angry one day, it's a great day because I am alive and able to feel anger. If I am sad, it's a great day because I am alive to feel sadness. If my day is wonderful, it's a great day because I am here to feel wonderful.

It is hard to explain, but each cancer journey I have taken, each scar and collapsed vein that I have from chemo and blood tests, the surgery and setbacks, the depression I dealt with, and those individuals that I have had to remove from life, made me the strong woman I am today. I am empowered. If you can embrace the essence of life, you will find the inner strength to power through this journey. Remember, you can only fight cancer from a position of strength and not from a position of weakness. What I do know and what my family will attest to is that I am not the same person I was two years ago. I am forever changed, and I am glad. I have a lot of "yesterdays," but not as many "tomorrows." My journey has taught me to lead a very rich life for whatever time I have left. I am a great deal wiser, thankfully.

Reflection 19: I have learned how delicate yet strong my body is. We can live and enjoy life on so few organs. We can live without a pancreas, spleen, a bile duct, one kidney, one lung, etc. Our liver can regenerate under certain conditions. It is a miracle. What a gift life is. Cherish it. You only get one life. Be kind to your body.

I found my strength through normalcy, which is why I went back to teaching aqua aerobics when only two months into my chemotherapy treatments. Normalcy provides those daily expectations that encourage you to keep moving. It may be doing what I do or it may be babysitting your grandchildren or volunteering three times a week for some organization. That is where you can derive a great deal of strength. If you have no purpose in your life, you will have no strength to draw from to fight this terrible and often fatal disease. Again, you can only fight cancer from a position of strength.

I also found strength in teaching my Parkinson's exercise class and subbing as an instructor for aqua multiple sclerosis. My new calling is my certification as a cancer exercise specialist. I believe these are some of the things that God had in mind for me. I can only have faith and believe.

You should always focus not on what you are facing but where you need to go. If you only focus on the cancer diagnosis, you cannot see beyond, and you will be unable to start your journey to healing and living life. You already know what is in front of you. It is more important to focus on where you want to get to.

Reflection 20: "In addition to your physical, mental and spiritual selves, there is your intuitive self. If at any time you question the medical information given you, the type of treatment recommended, or are just experiencing an uncomfortableness with your mental, physical or spiritual self, trust your intuitive self. It will guide you. Don't ignore it and find down the road that you could have, should have, would have if you only had trusted your intuition.

In summary, if you draw on your life's strengths, have faith, believe in yourself, surround yourself with supportive family and friends, teach yourself, embrace yourself, and address your weaknesses, you will be empowered to act as a self-advocate. Who better to advocate for you than you?

This is not the end for me. This journey is my new beginning. Quite frankly, I am loving my new life, and I hope you will love yours too.

About the Author

Leona knew that when she retired, she wanted to enter into a field where she could help people. As she left her career in the legal field behind, she stepped into the fitness industry. Leona had a sister born with learning disabilities in addition to health issues and took on the role of caregiver. It was through this experience she learned first-hand the importance of helping individuals who had various health problems or disabilities. Then one day, her whole life changed when diagnosed with the first of three primary cancers. She became overwhelmed with fighting this disease, balancing her life with her husband, dealing with depression, continuing in her role as caregiver, and finding her relationship with God. She learned very quickly that life is full of uncertainties and that nothing was as it seemed. But she also found a new beginning she could have never envisioned.

To learn more about Leona's plight, visit her website at sinkorswimthebook.com. There, you will also be able to visit her blog and even contact her.

CPSIA information can be obtained
at www.ICGtesting.com
Printed in the USA
BVHW061329020321
601496BV00012B/1726